Athabasca Seasons

Athabasca Seasons

A Memoir

Audrey Weldon Reid

Best wishes

Audrey Reid

Shoreline

Cover by Sarah Robinson
Edited by Andrea Belcham
Family photographs from the author's collection
Photos of the town and river from the Athabasca Archives
Photograph of the author, page 111, by Heather Kelly
Printed in Canada by AGMV Marquis

Published by Shoreline, 23 Ste-Anne
Ste-Anne-de-Bellevue, Quebec, Canada H9X 1L1
Phone/fax 514-457-5733
shoreline@sympatico.ca   www.shorelinepress.ca

Dépôt legal: National Library of Canada
et la Bibliothèque nationale du Québec

NATIONAL LIBRARY OF CANADA CATALOGUING IN
PUBLICATION DATA
Reid, Audrey Weldon
Athabasca seasons: a memoir / Audrey Weldon Reid
ISBN 1-896754-26-0
1.Reid, Audrey Weldon.
2.Athabasca River Region (Alta.) -Biography. I.Title.

FC3695.A85R44 2003   971.23'202'092   C2003-901867-9
F1079.A8R44 2003

Dedication

To my husband, Jack; our children, Carol and Rob;
our son-in-law, Frank, our granddaughters, Jaime and Kacie;
and my sister, Nan

To the memory of my parents, Robert and Annie Weldon;
my siblings, Dick, George, Ralph, and Marg;
and our little daughter, Donna.

Acknowledgements

I thank the following for their encouragement and advice:

Shirley Serviss, Eunice Scarfe, Judy Schultz, Allison Kydd,
Norm Sacuta, and JackBilsland

Jack, my husband, and Rob, our son, for spending so many hours
proofreading my stories

Nan, my sister, who helped me remember the events described in
the stories

My writer friends Ardith Trudzik, Sue Marxheimer and Joyce
Harries for giving me the confidence to write

Anne Kruger for her wonderful drawings

Andrea Belcham and Judy Isherwood of Shoreline

Author's Note

This book is my way of preserving my memories and understanding my life. I have attempted to be faithful to the truth; where my memory has failed, however, my imagination fills in the blanks. I hope there are not too many inaccuracies in my stories.

Several of these stories have appeared in the *Edmonton Journal* and the Alberta Retired Teachers Association's *News and Views*. The stories, "Putting on the Dog" and "Our Last Camping Trip," won third and first prizes in the 1999 and 2001 Alberta Senior Games respectively. In 1995 Grant MacEwan College awarded me the Laurie Allen Award for some of this work.

Contents

Prologue

I have always looked back on my childhood with fondness. My memories of this period are like the Athabasca River, which winds its way near the land that was my family's homestead in Alberta. In the summer the river is clear, flowing gently between sloping banks. My pleasant reminiscences are like the serene river when a slight breeze ruffles it, making the sunlight sparkle on the surface.

Yet the river is not always so: in the spring it becomes a raging creature. Jagged chunks of ice, pushed along by the strong current, crash together in violent booms. The water is dark then, and choked with broken branches. It is in the river's murky depths that I have hidden my most painful memories.

Now I am ready to brave the river in all its moods. This is the story of my childhood on the Athabasca, as it and I went from spring to summer to fall to winter and around again. The seasons of the Athabasca appear in my stories, not only as the backdrop, but as a sort of timeline for my early years.

Early Arrival

We lived by the Athabasca River, and the river ruled our lives. Its strength and its belligerent nature fashioned my entry into this world. The tale of my birth has been told many times by many different family members. When I was young, it thrilled me to listen to the story; I have kept it bright in my memory through the many years of my life.

In late winter, when the ice on the river was thick enough to hold both vehicles and horses, we would haul our provisions from the town of Athabasca across the river to our farm. For a week or two every spring, when the ice broke apart and the river let loose its strength and anger, we would be trapped at home. Fragile little boats or a rickety little cage would allow for a precarious crossing only if the need was dire, as it was when I was born.

I was due in May, in harmony with the river's rhythm. By then, the Athabasca's fury would have subsided, and the ferry would be able to cross in calm water. Mom was to be in the town hospital for her confinement period. Being a contrary and impatient child even then, however, I started clamouring for release from my little cocoon one day in mid-April.

Mom began to worry. A city girl born and raised in the Maritimes, she had accompanied Dad to this remote spot in the Albertan wilderness without protest, somehow dealing with all the challenges of pioneer life with humour and fortitude. Yet her last child had been a difficult birth: only the doctor's skill had saved the baby. This memory made her uncharacteristically nervous when the time came for me to be born. All of her other children had been born in a hospital with a doctor in attendance; to give birth in this isolated house with no amenities and no doctor at hand was beyond even her power to handle with equanimity. So she turned to prayer, her usual solace in times of trouble.

9

"Dear God, please help me," she prayed. But she was realistic enough to know that she had to try her best to help God help her.

"Bob, come to the house, quick!" she called to Dad. He dropped the pump handle he had been holding and came running. "The baby's coming early," she said breathlessly. "You'll have to get Dr. Myers. Don't take the car, take Nellie." Our car was a rattletrap, and Nellie was the fastest horse Dad owned. "Stop at the Gormans' on the way and telephone the doctor," she said. The doctor would then be able to cross the river in a cage or boat to meet Dad on our side of the river. "Please hurry!"

Dad asked steadily, "Are you sure the baby is coming now, Annie? It's early, isn't it? This could be false labour."

"No, Bob," she answered breathlessly. "I've had five children; I know what real labour is. You must hurry and get the doctor."

"All right," he said, firmly. "I'll go fast as I can. We should be back in two hours. Try and hang on." He leaned over and gave her a strong hug. "I love you," he said.

He led Nellie into the yard, leaped onto her back and set off at a gallop. Another saddle horse loped along beside him for the doctor to ride on the return trip. My mother knew it was five miles to the telephone and another five to the doctor; and then the doctor might not want to brave the river, for he would have to climb into the wobbly little cage that teetered on a line across the water, or he would have to cross in a fragile boat, weaving his way between chunks of ice.

Mom took her Bible and murmured a prayer. "Heavenly Father," she intoned, "please let Dr. Myers be at home and let him be brave enough to come." The labour pains were growing stronger and closer together. I must be calm, she reasoned, putting aside the book. Perhaps it really is only false labour; besides, Bob will soon be back with the doctor.

The two promised hours passed and the pains increased in force and frequency. Oh, dear God, she thought, I'm going to have this baby all by myself with only a bunch of scared kids to help. This frightening realization spurred her into action. She called her eldest son into the house.

"Dick, saddle Jill and ride to Mrs. Brown's," she instructed him firmly. Mrs. Brown was an old woman who had helped several local farmwives through their birthing times. Though the woman was reputed to be part witch, Mom knew that any help was better than no help at all. "Ride fast, dear, and say I need her." Dick knew about babies, unlike his younger siblings, and he took his mission very seriously: he caught a horse, bounded onto its back without a saddle and galloped away to be his mother's saviour.

An hour later he returned, flushed and sweating. Old Mrs. Brown bounced along behind him on the horse, clutching his waist with her bony hands. Her hair stuck up in woolly, grey tufts, her front tooth was missing and she wore a ragged, brown sweater wrapped around her body; at that moment, she seemed to be very much the witch.

She entered the house, being rather spry for a lady of her age, and started calling out orders to Dick. "Bring me some sheets and tear them into pieces. Boil a kettle of water." She spotted George, the next eldest child, and told him to take the others to the barn loft to play. "I don't want them underfoot," she said.

"Is that you, Mrs. Brown?" Mom called out from her bed, her voice weak with relief. "But where's Bob?" she asked.

"He ain't back yet, honey," the old lady replied, arranging the things that Dick had found for her. "Just give over now and relax. After all, it's yer sixth babe, so you've had lots of practice. Easy now, and you'll do real good!" She touched my mother's distended abdomen and then brought her hand to my mother's head, gently weaving her rough fingers through my mother's tangled hair. "Dick," she said quietly, "go now and look after the other kids." Dick scooted obediently outside.

"Oh, Mrs. Brown, the pains are awful," Mom panted.

"Just push, dearie. Push as hard as you can," said the midwife.

11

Mom screamed, for the pain seemed unbearable; then, remembering the children, she stifled her voice.

"The baby's on its way now. Give one more strong push. Good for you, Annie. It's coming now: there's the head! Lots of hair. Here comes the body. Yep, it's a girl! Skinny little thing, but she's here, red and scrawny." Mrs. Brown lifted me up to give me a slap on my bum and I emitted a sharp little wail. Humming to herself, she cut the umbilical cord and washed me. Finding no baby blanket at hand, she wrapped me in her own brown sweater.

"Don't she jest beat all?" She grinned as she patted me and handed me to Mom.

Mom smiled through her tears as she held me close and grasped the old lady's hand. "Thank you, Mrs. Brown," she said, "You're truly a good midwife." This "witch" is really an angel, she thought, as she drifted off into exhausted sleep.

When Dad and the doctor finally reached the house, small mewling sounds met their ears. "Guess I'm too late!" said Dr. Myers. "Did I cross that raging water and ice for nothing?" he asked, feigning annoyance.

"Looks that way," said Dad, embarrassed. Then, he smiled as he picked up the brown, howling bundle, and handed him to Dr. Myers.

Mrs. Brown said, "I'll make you some tea before you head back." Dad and the doctor drank it before they left.

Later, my brother Ralph heard my cries and ventured into the house. "Do we have kittens?" he asked.

School Days

It was a glorious September day. The sun warmed the world and the wind whisked across the road, mingling the scent of ripe grain with the musty smells of high-bush cranberries and decaying grasses. It was on this day that I was to start school.

I skipped along the path, so excited I could hardly keep from running. My big sister, Nan, strode along behind me, calling out for me to wait. I stopped and kicked at the dirt on the road, stirring up a little cloud of dust that settled on my new black patent leather shoes. I bent down and brushed them until they were clean and shiny again, then rubbed my dusty hands on my underpants.

I had been waiting for this day for a long time. During the previous year, when I was only five, Mom often packed a lunch for me and let me walk a quarter of a mile up the road with Nan on her trek to school. Once Nan left me, I would walk back home. There, I would sit at the dining-room table, drawing, colouring and reading simple stories to Mom, until the scents of my bologna sandwich and ripe apple tempted me to eat my packed lunch. I often dreamed of a future in which I would be old enough to go to school; in my imagination, the teacher always smiled at me and praised me for my efforts. At the end of my pretend school day, I would go outside to play with my dog or chat with Dad.

A new world was opening up for me as I walked beside Nan on this particular morning: I was truly going to school! I looked down at my pink dress with its matching coat that Mom had sewn for me. She had made it from Aunt Bessie's old suit turned inside out. It was beautiful, and I had knee-high socks to match it. The patent leather shoes were a bonus: they had been ordered from the Eaton's catalogue after much pleading on my part. I had stood on a piece of paper while Mom carefully outlined my feet with a pencil, and then we had sent the patterns off with the order to Winnipeg. The shoes finally came by mail. When I put them on and danced around the living room, they sparkled. (They were really only for church, but I was allowed to wear them for this special occasion.)

Nan and I arrived at school, opened the heavy door and entered the world of my dreams. The room smelled of the sweeping compound that was sprinkled on the oiled wooden floor; of lunches filled with boiled eggs and garlic sausage; of cow barns (for many kids had milking chores to do before school); and of the dusty paper in the well-thumbed readers.

Nan was in the ninth grade at the time, so she sat down at a desk in the back of the room. The teacher looked down at me grimly and pointed to a desk in the front row. "Sit there," she commanded. I had never seen anyone look so cross! She had black hair and straight black eyebrows that grew so close together they almost touched above her nose.

She dumped a box of tattered cardboard letters on my desk.

"Find the letters that spell your name and the name of the school," she said brusquely. "Spell my name, as well: I am Miss Alexander." She marched off to the big kids. I started sifting through the dusty letters, but I was slow at finding the ones I needed. I had not yet finished forming my name when she appeared above me and stared down at the mess of letters.

"What's the matter with you? Why haven't you finished?" she demanded, sweeping my letters into their box. I was not even allowed to finish my first task.

The day was filled with other disappointments. Nothing I did seemed to please the angry lady. The only pleasure I had was in playing outside at recess, but even in this I had to restrain myself because I was afraid of soiling my pretty dress.

At the end of the day, Miss Alexander announced in her sharp voice, "The first grade is now dismissed. Take your things from the cloakroom and go straight home. Don't let me catch any of you hanging around the schoolyard." I looked at Nan for guidance

14

guidance; her usual confidence seemed cowed by the presence of the teacher, however, and she only stared down at her desk.

I stepped out the door, clutching my yellow Burns Lard lunch pail. Now what should I do, I wondered. Mom had told me to wait for Nan. Two miles was much too far for me to walk alone. I thought of the big red bull with its long horns, in the field that we had to cut across on our way home. He was sure to run after me! I was afraid to stay, but I was more afraid to set off alone.

I sneaked around to the back of the school and sat quietly on my lunch pail, hoping no one would see me. After a few moments, I opened my pail, took out the remains of a peanut butter sandwich and began to munch on it.

Suddenly, a big boy named Herbie appeared from around the corner and marched past me toward the outhouses. As he was returning to the school, he looked at me and grinned nastily. "Didn't you hear the teacher tell you to go home? I'm going to tell on you!" he said with a smirk and walked off. I sat there trembling.

A few minutes later, Miss Alexander loomed above me. "You are a disobedient child. Come inside and wait in the cloakroom. I will deal with you later," she promised. I went inside and huddled among the coats and lunch pails. Tears coursed down my cheeks. I had never been given the strap, and I realized that this punishment might be awaiting me. At last she sent the other kids home. I peered through the window hoping to see Nan; she had left the schoolyard and was sitting on a stone by the road.

"Come here!" Miss Alexander commanded. Her black eyebrows came together in a fierce frown as she pulled a leather strap from the top drawer of her desk.

"I hear that your mother told you to wait for your sister. Well, you'd better learn right now that *I*, not your mother, make the rules around here. Now hold out your hand!" *Smack!* Down came the first blow of the strap. "Do you understand me?" she demanded, glowering down at me. *Smack!* Down came the second one. Another two resounding swats were delivered to ensure my understanding. My hand throbbed and my great expectations crumbled. This was not the glorious world of school that I had been so eagerly anticipating.

"Go!" she said, giving me a push out the door. I found Nan by the roadside and we trudged home while I blubbered out my story. I declared that when I grew up, I would be a teacher - and unlike Miss Alexander, *I* would keep my students happy.

At home I announced that I would never again venture into the schoolhouse. Unfortunately, Mom squelched this plan, informing me that I would have to go back and try my best to humour Miss Alexander. "Smile at her and do as she says," she suggested.

The school year continued in a similarly unpleasant way, with that old strap always at the ready to punish me for any infraction of the rules. Many mornings I tried to feign illness by pinching my cheeks until they looked red and feverish, but this ruse seldom succeeded. The forbidding Miss Alexander never showed a glimmer of warmth toward any of the children in her charge, and she failed to display even a trace of enjoyment in her tasks. Thankfully, the dreadful year finally came to an end and I was set free for the summer.

I soon heard that Miss Alexander had been dismissed because it had been discovered that she was really "Mrs. Nelson." Apparently, she had kept her marriage secret for fear of losing her job. While I did wonder for a moment if the necessity for secrecy was what had made her so cranky, I was only too glad to be rid of her. The long, lovely summer stretched out before me, and I was sure that the next year would be better. I hoped that school would finally be the place of my imaginings, a place for me to excel and be praised.

A Coat for a Pencil

Though poverty marked the lives of many during the 1930s, Mom managed to shield me from the prevailing mood of bleakness. She made lovely clothes for us, beautifully crafted and sewn with meticulous care and attention. Sometimes she spent some of her hoarded cash on material from the store; or she might turn material from old clothes inside out and make pretty outfits for us. The fabrics on the inside of these older clothes were still vibrant, and to them she added splashes of colour in the forms of collars, cuffs or linings. Her creations rivalled anything that could be bought in the stores or ordered from the Eaton's catalogue.

For special events like the Christmas concert, she bought taffeta or organdy, and produced frilly pink, turquoise or mauve dresses with crisp white crinolines that made the skirts stand out and swirl around me. These clothes made me feel special and much loved. No indication of the poverty that was the norm pierced my rosy view of the world.

I remember the attractive outfit I wore on the first day of school: it is as clear a vision in my mind as the clothes I wore yesterday. Mom had received a pink coat of fine wool from her sister Bessie, whose affluence may have engendered a little envy in Mom, but seemed only a boon to me. Mom pulled the threads from all the seams and cut pieces for a small coat and dress, using a pattern she had made herself. She bought plain pink gabardine for the collar and cuffs of the coat and big pink buttons for the closing. She even spent some of her small amount of cash on pink socks and black patent leather shoes for me.

On the first day that I donned my coat for school, I was allowed to wear my new shoes to go with my attractive outfit. I skipped along the road to class, feeling like a princess. It seemed a wonderful day. The wool coat was warm and I could wear it happily until late fall by wearing an extra sweater inside it to ward off

17

change into last year's blanket cloth snowsuit.

I had a classmate named Jessie who came to school day after day in a threadbare sweater, her red and cracked skin peeping out from ragged holes at the elbows. She would arrive at school blue and shaking from the cold. Each day I secretly looked at her, and couldn't help but sense her chill.

One day she came to school with a scarf wrapped around her spindly body; it was the only barrier between her and the frosty Alberta air. I felt so sorry for her that I had to do something. I offered her my pink coat, confident that Mom could sew me a new one with little trouble.

Jessie looked at me suspiciously and said with a sniff, "You think I'm poor? Maybe I am, but I don't want your charity!" She stomped away.

"Well, then," I said, as I followed her in a circle around the school, "I'll trade you my coat for something of yours. What do you have to trade?"

The beginnings of a grin lit up her face, and she fished a yellow pencil from her pocket. She held it out, its well-chewed eraser pointing toward me. "Here, you can have my pencil for your coat. That's fair, isn't it?" she said with a sudden, big smile.

"Okay," I answered quickly. I grabbed her pencil, threw my coat at her, and took off for home. The road grew longer and the wind grew colder as I trudged my way along the two-mile trek. As I walked, I wondered what Mom would say, what material she would use to make me a new coat and how much work it would be for her. The wind whistled through my flimsy sweater and my steps slowed as I plodded slowly home.

As I neared the farm, I saw Mom hanging out clothes in the back yard. I ventured hesitantly toward her. What if she made me get my coat back from Jessie? Thoughts of the humiliation that would arise from this dreadful situation filled my mind. Mom dropped the damp clothes she was holding into the basket and put her arms around my shivering shoulders.

"What happened to your coat, dear?" she asked. "Did you forget it at school? Surely you couldn't be that absentminded, could you? You're chilled to the bone." I hugged her close, sobbing out my sorry tale.

"I traded it for a pencil," I said, taking the yellow item from my pocket. I pulled back to look at her and judge her reaction. "Isn't that fair?" I asked hopefully. I told her that Jessie had no coat at all, and I said that I was sure she, my dear, kind mother, could easily make me a new one. She led me into the house, planted me by the fire and sat in her rocker beside me. She seemed to be blinking back tears.

"Are you mad at me, Mom?" I pleaded.

"Well, dear," she answered, "I'll have to make you another coat, and it will take some time because I don't have any warm material to use right now. You'll have to wear your snowsuit until I save enough money to buy some new material. But I'm not angry with you. In fact, I think you're a generous child, and I'm proud of you."

Jessie wore my coat all winter, though she never showed me any gratitude for my gift - she never even glanced in my direction. Looking back at this event after the many years that have passed, I can imagine the despair that Mom must have felt at the prospect of having to sew a new coat, for her days were filled with chores already. She had created such a beautiful outfit and dressed me in it so proudly. Yet no word of scolding ever fell onto my shoulders. I now marvel at her tolerance and understanding. A new coat, a brown one with a red lining, appeared for me on Christmas morning.

Silent Night

Christmas was coming. Miss Nancekivell, my second grade teacher, had assigned parts for our school concert. The Christmas concert was a wonderful event and certainly the most exciting thing that happened in the whole year.

Our class spent an hour each day preparing costumes and practicing our parts. The program was to start with "O Canada," of course. The first and second graders were to sing "Away in a Manger." The Christmas pageant was to come after that. I was to be a sheep and say "ba-a, ba-a" in a sheep-like voice. My animal was cut out of grey manila tag, with black for the ears and nose, and was to be strapped to my side with binder twine. I was to crawl onto the stage, trying to keep my body hidden behind it. I'd asked to play the Virgin Mary, but Miss Nancekivell told me Dorothy was getting that part because she was blonde.

"Have you ever heard of a Virgin Mary with red hair?" she asked with a smile as she patted my head. I couldn't follow this logic, as I figured the Virgin Mary could have hair that was any colour.

After the pageant, the fourth and fifth grade girls were to dance the Irish lilt in their green crêpe-paper skirts and their white blouses with black crêpe-paper sashes. Black shoelaces were sewn in a criss-cross pattern on the front of their blouses, and they had green paper bows in their hair. They were supposed to wear black shoes, but some of the girls didn't have any; Muriel wore her brother's boots and Jilly had to wear her moccasins. I was amazed at how well the girls danced, holding their bodies stiff while their feet flew this way and that, making the leather soles of their shoes click loudly on the wooden stage.

The big kids were to do a dance called the Virginia Reel, in which they swirled back and forth across the stage. During practices, a rickety gramophone scratched out the music. For the real concert, however, Daniel Goodwin was to make magical music on his fiddle. He was always dressed in black breeches and a red Mackinaw shirt, and he wore a merry grin as he sawed the bow back and forth across the strings, banging his feet on the floor until the dust flew up in clouds.

Next, the Artym kids were to play and sing, as they did each year. They ran through a practice to show what they could do. Walter played the guitar, Gloria played the mandolin, while Emily sang one song in English and one in Ukrainian. I didn't understand the Ukrainian song, though I was thrilled by her high, sweet voice. The English song was "Star of the East," and when Emily sang out "bearing gifts, they travel so far," Miss Nancekivell stopped her and said it was supposed to be "traver so far." Emily didn't pay any attention, and I didn't blame her—who had ever heard of the word "traver"? Looking back, I think she must have meant "traverse."

The recitations were to follow this. In the first grade I had performed a short one that I called "The Elephunk," where everyone had laughed at my poor pronunciation. I dearly hoped that I'd get another chance. Sure enough, the teacher looked straight at me and asked, "Do you think you can learn to recite 'The Night before Christmas'?" I hopped from one foot to the other with glee.

The big day finally arrived. We trooped with our props and costumes from the school to the community hall for our dress rehearsal. All of the kids wore what passed as their best clothes ("best" meant washed and in relatively good condition). Billy and Milton, however, wore what they always wore, flannel shirts and overalls stiffened by dirt and they didn't smell any better than usual. The girls came with their hair done up in rags like shiny little sausages. On ordinary days, most kids had stringy hair like dirty straw; for the Christmas concert, all the kids had washed their hair, even those children in dirty overalls.

Mom always made me a new dress for the school concerts, and this year was no exception. I wore my black, strapped summer shoes instead of my usual moccasins. My feet hurt in the

21

summer shoes, for I had to scrunch up my toes to make them fit. I wouldn't get a new pair of shoes until the next summer, so I rubbed Vaseline on the old patent leather ones until they shone.

After decorating the hall and the tree, we started the official dress rehearsal. I joined in the songs and belted out "Away in a Manger" and "Good King Wenceslas" with all my power. When we finished, Miss Nancekivell moved quietly up beside me, patted my shoulder and whispered, "Would you just pretend you're singing, and not make any noise? You're flat."

I was stunned. What did she mean I was flat? Of course I was! I was only eight and skinny as a board; what did that have to do with singing? Then Ellen nudged me and hissed, "It means she wants you to shut up because you can't sing!" My face flamed with anger and shame. Oh, how I hated Ellen at that moment, and how I hated Miss Nancekivell even more. My joy was gone.

At seven the concert began, with all the big people watching. For the little children's song, I stood in the back row mouthing the words and looking down at my feet. The unfairness of it all! Yet when it came time for my recitation, my spirits rose. I walked up onto the empty stage in my new turquoise dress, knowing every word of the poem, as I had practiced it with Mom.

When I came to the part about Santa "laying a finger aside of his nose," the door at the back of the hall opened to reveal my big sister, who had been away at school all year. I was surprised and excited, and couldn't wait to speak with her.

"Hi, Margaret," I shouted, waving both arms in case she didn't see me. Then I returned to the part in my recitation about Santa's nod, and finished the presentation with a "Merry Christmas to all and to all a good night!" I hopped off the stage to laughter and applause and ran through the crowd to give Margaret a hug.

The next item was the pageant, which went fairly well, except that some of the kids forgot their lines and the teacher had to whisper to them several times. I managed to keep behind my manila sheep most of the time. The big kids swished across the stage

22

in the Virginia Reel, keeping perfect time. The final item was the Irish Lilt, and it was proceeding successfully until Rosie turned around to reveal her uncovered blue bloomers for everyone to see. Her crêpe paper skirt had come undone and was dragging on the floor. When she saw it tangled under her feet, she turned red and walked backward off the stage. Everyone giggled. Poor Rosie!

When at last the concert was over, we all lined up on the stage to bow for the audience. The concert must have been good, because their applause was tremendous.

At that moment, Santa walked in the door with his pack (he had to come that way, we were told, because there was no chimney in the hall, and anyone could see that he was too fat to come through the stovepipe). He called our names and handed each of us a bag of nuts and candy, with a Japanese orange on top. Mr. Goodwin played his fiddle again, and two other men played guitars while the big people danced. The babies were bundled up and laid to sleep next to the cakes and sandwiches in the cloakroom.

I was sleepy when they finally played "Home Sweet Home" and the food was passed around. Later, my family piled two deep into our old car and we drove off; I fell asleep on someone's knee. At last, we arrived home. I couldn't wait for the day when the real Santa Claus would come.

The humiliation of being barred from singing at the concert was soon outshone by the joy of having Margaret home, and of participating in such a happy, family Christmas.

The Wrath of the Athabasca River

My father had settled his family on a piece of land north of the town of Athabasca, Alberta. Between our homestead and the town ran the Athabasca River. This river was wide, strong and temperamental, and it isolated or accommodated us according to its whims. During the summer, the water was temperate and friendly: a ferry on cables plied its way across the river. In the winter, several feet of ice provided a strong bridge to the town.

In the spring it was different. The river broke free with fierce and unrelenting force, imposing its will upon the people who tried to cohabit with it. Choked with ice, it became a giant, living creature bent on destruction. It raged along, carrying jagged chunks of ice that crashed into each other and pounded up onto the banks with a terrifying roar that echoed through the town.

During this season, a flimsy creation called "the cage" by the local inhabitants, swayed its precarious way across the river, suspended in the air by a mere cable. I suppose this contraption was the pioneer version of a gondola, but it bore a closer resemblance to a crate for hauling livestock. Six to eight passengers standing erect, each with a small bundle of goods stowed at his or her feet, could be accommodated at a time.

On such a spring day, Dad took me to town as a treat for my eighth birthday. This risky action seems strange in retrospect, but as we had to live with this river in all its moods, we made the best of our situation. Dad made his purchases and I selected a birthday present, a small set of pink china dishes; then we were ready to go home. Dad took several loads across the river in the cage, and prepared to return and take me over on his final crossing.

As I waited, clutching my box of dishes, the river erupted in a new fury, churning up mountains of ice and challenging anyone to interfere with it. The little cage would be ripped from its cable and would surely plunge its passengers to their deaths if it tempted the violent river. I remember my feeling of desolation as

24

I waved forlornly at my father, who stood helplessly on the opposite bank. Overcome by terror, I thought of spending the night alone amongst the masses of ice on the shore. Lost in my frightening dream of the hours that awaited me, I failed to notice the time slipping away. When I looked up, Dad had disappeared from sight, and I was truly alone.

Huddled on a piece of driftwood, I awaited my fate. Would wolves come and devour me? I was sure they were howling. How near were they? Or would some hobo from town come to kidnap me? There were a lot of tramps around the streets of Athabasca in their raggedy clothes; I prayed they would sense I wasn't worth much. Perhaps I would just freeze to death; I was chilled to the bone already. Pulling my coat tightly around me, I tried to draw some warmth from the box of dishes I clutched to my chest.

After what seemed like hours, the crunch of footsteps on ice aroused me from my bout of self-pity, and I looked up to see a pair of long black legs silhouetted against the grey-white hills of ice. I looked farther and farther up, past a black coat, to a white collar and a gentle, smiling face. Was it God Himself, come to rescue me? I had certainly been praying enough! Then I recognized the figure as Mr. Hockin, our kindly minister. He smiled and extended his hand.

"Your dad phoned me from the ferryman's house," he said. "You're to come home with me until the river calms down and he can get across again."

The telephone. I hadn't thought of that. I was saved! With comforting words, Mr. Hockin led me to his house, where I spent the night happily ensconced in the warmth of his family.

By morning, the river had subsided and the intrepid little cage was in business again and trundled Dad and me over the water. Though relatively calm, the river still threatened to become belligerent. When we finally arrived home, the whole family was waiting to welcome me with a big birthday cake, and I was the heroine of the hour.

25

Hunting for Pennies

Something glinted like silver under the wooden sidewalk. I picked up a little stick and poked at it through the planks. It was a nickel. Prodding it this way and that, I finally scraped away enough of the soil for it to slide out. I dusted it off on my dress and added it to my little bundle. In my pocket was fifteen cents; one more nickel would get me into the movie theatre. I'd have to keep looking.

I had come to this situation by putting my faith in my big brother, Ralph, even though I knew he was not very dependable. He was tall, handsome and so interested in girls and in his own activities that he hadn't much time for an eight-year-old kid. On this day, however, he smiled and asked me if I'd like to go to town with him. What excitement that promised! Athabasca was ten miles from our farm and it held untold pleasures. I pictured the big pink ice-cream cone sign that hung on wires outside the Royal Café. My mouth watered at the thought, and I could almost smell the sweet strawberry dessert it advertised.

Mom had given me a whole quarter to spend. I knotted it in my hanky, stowed it in the pocket of my dress and hopped joyfully into the car. The old jalopy wheezed and gasped and then off we clattered, chug-chugging our way to town, spitting up a trail of grey dust in our wake. As we bounced along the rutted road, I planned my purchases. Twenty-five cents meant five different five-cent items. I hoped Ralph would stay in town long enough for me to enjoy the day.

Ralph let me off in the town centre and I dashed straight to the Royal Café. My first purchase was a wonderful ice-cream cone; I derived joy from every lick, right down to the crunchy cone. Next I bought a package of chewing gum and a chocolate bar. Eating little bits of the bar, I wandered up and down the streets. The rich flavour and nutty texture of the candy flooded over me and spread to my very toes as I crunched the nuts and let the dark chocolate melt in my mouth.

Putting some of it in my pocket for later, I ventured into Mr. Falconer's hardware store, where the smell of kerosene filled the air. I looked at a set of children's china dishes, more lavish than the one I had, and admired a big, beautifully dressed doll with bright blue eyes and shiny yellow hair. Though I longed to touch her glossy curls, I didn't dare try. I left the hardware store and walked bravely into the grocery shop.

"What are you doing all by yourself?" Mr. Redden asked with a smile. Too shy to answer properly, I mumbled a vague answer and made a hasty exit. The afternoon slipped away as I wandered from store to store.

The clock on the post office told me that three hours had passed since I'd last seen Ralph, waving and calling out, "See ya!" as the jalopy clattered off. It was getting late and I was becoming frightened. Where was he? Why had he left me alone so long? I couldn't keep walking the streets. If I found another five pennies, I would be allowed into the movie hall, where I'd be warm and safe. I managed to collect three more pennies, which left me only two cents short. Maybe they'd let me in with that much if I pretended I didn't understand money. With that idea in mind, I climbed the dusty, creaking stairs to the hall above Parkers' General Store and presented my eighteen cents with my best smile.

"Dear," said the lady at the wicket, "it costs twenty cents for kids."

"Oh, I didn't know," I stammered. My cheeks burned.

"That's okay," she said kindly, "you can go in, anyway."

I slunk thankfully into the dark hall, nearly overcome by the aroma of hot, buttered popcorn. Having no money, however, I tried not to think about it. My chocolate was long gone, so I chewed noisily on my gum. The screen flickered into life and I was soon lost in the adventures of Lassie, which shut off my troubles for a while.

27

Eventually, the movie ended and I was swept down the stairs with the crowd. I peered up and down the street, certain that Ralph would be looking for me. It would serve him right if he had been searching for me frantically all this time! Yet, there was no sign of him or our car. I walked up and down every street and looked in every store window - he was nowhere to be found.

I wandered into the hardware store again, but the items on display had lost their attraction and the smell of kerosene made me feel sick. I walked back to the grocery store as Mr. Redden knew Dad. Maybe he would be able to help me, but he was pulling down the window blinds.

"We're closing now, so you'll have to leave," he said, patting my head. "You'd better go find your parents." I slipped out and hurried back to the main street.

I was feeling real terror then. It was growing dark and I was alone. What would I do if Ralph never came back? I could gladly have killed him, and could hardly wait to tell Mom and Dad. This made me feel a little better.

The smell of hamburgers and French fries from the Chinese restaurant nearly bowled me over, but my hunger pangs were making me forget my fear and anger. I passed Fix's Garage where the men, in greasy overalls that smelled of gasoline, were closing up shop. I heard the big doors came clanging down. Across the street, closer to the river, loud laughter drifted out from the beer parlour. Better not go down that way, I warned myself: who knew what dark doings went on in there? I watched a family stow boxes in their truck and then drive away. No one was on the street now: I felt utterly alone.

I crossed the street, crept into the entranceway of the drugstore and sat on the dusty wooden steps. I cried a little, but as there was no one to see me and offer condolences, I soon stopped and huddled in the dark to await my sad fate. At last, a car came edging slowly down the street toward me. It drew closer. Ralph pulled up, opened the door with a grin, to see a young girl come running and throw herself into the seat beside him.

28

"I went to the lake and forgot about the time," he said, as though his treacherous act didn't amount to much. "Did you get your ice-cream cone?"

His ignorance was too much for me. Safely inside the car, I let my anger fly with full force. I pounded his chest, head and arms with my fists.

"I'm telling on you, you big meany! Just you wait, you big meany!" ("meany" was the worst name I could think of to call him right then). I cried all the way home, as much out of relief as of anger.

When we arrived home at last, I had hugs and a warm supper before being sent off to sleep. Before settling into bed, I saw Ralph coming out of our parents' bedroom with a very red face and a sober expression. He was extra nice to me for quite a while.

Childhood Beds

I've had a great variety of beds during my life, but those of my childhood were unique, each a tribute to my mother's resourcefulness. At seven years old, the youngest child in a house brimming over with assorted family members, guests, boarders, hired hands, dogs, and cats, I was shifted from bed to bed regularly.

In our house there were four bedrooms, each with a double bed; each bed had been allocated before my birth. First, there was the boys' bed (for three brothers, but the eldest was often away). Next, there was the girls' bed - my older sisters had dibs on that one. My parents' bed was theirs without question. Finally, there was the teacher's bed. As our boarder, she had the luxury of a whole bed to herself, though she shared it in emergencies.

My sleeping place depended on three factors: the current density of the house's population, the degree of Mom's exhaustion and my sisters' pleasure or displeasure with my recent behaviour. If I was in a state of relative approval in their eyes, I was allowed to sleep with them in their narrow bed. We would snuggle together, resentments forgotten and sins forgiven, and sleep against one another like "stacked spoons," as we were fond of saying. In the event of a desperate situation, I was lodged with the teacher, who taught me every day. This made me very nervous. Mom cautioned me to be sure that I was very clean, to splash on cologne, and not to wiggle in my sleep.

On the last occasion of this particular sleeping arrangement, I awoke to find myself awash in a warm puddle of my own making, which, to my horror, was seeping inexorably toward the sleeping form of the esteemed teacher. I jumped out of the bed and escaped to the outhouse, where I sat alone with my shame. When I was thoroughly chilled, I went inside to wash and put on dry clothes. Mom did not admonish me, but simply apologized to the teacher on my behalf. Oh, the humiliation I suffered in class that day when I had to face my prim teacher.

Another place where I often slept was in our living room, on a rickety contraption called a Winnipeg couch, which unfolded into a bed. It was from here that I could watch the night-time family events unfold. If a guest was occupying this couch I was relegated to sleeping on two large chairs pushed together. At other times I slept on a cot covered by a tick made of flour sacks sewn together and stuffed with straw. When new, a tick was soft and comfortable; as it aged, however, it grew hard and lumpy, and its straw poked through to prick me as I slept.

My cot was placed in various spots, sometimes under the front windows, where it was cold and draughty, sometimes behind the big wood stove, where it was warm and cozy, and sometimes in the so-called bathroom. In the bathroom I shared my sleeping space with an old tin tub and a washstand that held a pitcher and a bowl. I was not fond of this spot and was put there only under vehement protest.

I have never felt deprived for lacking a bedroom or bed of my own; on the contrary, my memories of my childhood beds are pleasant ones. These makeshift beds are symbols of belonging, not deprivation. My family always managed to find a place for me.

Life in the Log House

Recently, I came across an old snapshot of our parents standing with all of us by our farmhouse. As I was growing up, this house was the centre of my very small and insulated world. Because the farmhouse was so geographically isolated, we created our own community within its walls. Although it was usually crammed with an untidy clutter of objects and a hodgepodge of varied activities, it embodied comfort and stability for me.

Our house, though large, was simple. Cedar siding had been applied to the exterior of the house to cover the logs. Its structure was quite typical of the homes built on the Prairies at that time. Our father devoted his financial resources to farm equipment: drills, seeders, binders, and combines, rather than home improvements.

The kitchen was small and cramped, too crowded for any meals to be eaten there. It was steamy and hot in the summer, cozy and pleasant in the winter. Against one wall stood a big table where bread, pies and cakes were prepared for baking. Under the table there was a large metal bread bin that was filled to the brim on baking days; it gradually emptied as the week wore on. A black and silver cream separator occupied one corner of the kitchen. It had two arms that spread upward and a big bowl that held the milk; after we poured the milk into the bowl, the separator would spin out the dairy components. Skimmed milk emerged from one spout and cream came out of the other.

In another corner, a messy pile of split wood, fuel for the ever-smouldering kitchen fire, scattered its chips and bark across the floor. Against another wall there stood a huge cupboard of kitchen supplies: dishes, baking tools, tea, coffee, sugar, and flour filled its wooden shelves. It had once been painted dark green and because of this had always been called the "green cupboard." For many years I did not realize that this name included a literal colour and thought that every kitchen had a "greencupboard."

32

Just outside the kitchen was a trap door that led into a cool cellar where root vegetables were stored in sand. This storehouse contained a bounty of foods. Shelf after shelf lined the walls, loaded with jars of colourful preserved fruit that stood shoulder-to-shoulder quite proudly, promising a year of delicious desserts. Boxes of apples and oranges wrapped in crinkly green paper filled the air with their tempting aromas.

The living room was large and square, with the bedrooms and kitchen adjoining two of its walls. It was in the living room that the life of the home ebbed and flowed. The big oak dining table was the heart of the house. Eight places had to be set for the family when we were all present, but there was always an additional assortment of hired hands and "guests" to seat. These guests would come and stay for months at a time, as my parents could never bring themselves to hint that anyone was unwelcome. Large, steaming bowls of potatoes or other available vegetables, meat, and eggs were the table staples, along with fragrant home-made bread. Mom sat at the end of the table nearest the kitchen, an arrangement that allowed her to jump up to bring refilled bowls to the table.

Dad presided in dignity at the other end of the table. From this position, he expounded enthusiastically on a wide variety of subjects; that is, if he could get the attention of the boisterous diners. He liked to give talks on the ways in which the government could stimulate the economy and draw the country out of the Depression.

Once, one of the hired hands, who felt a reply to one of Dad's speeches was required, added the comment, "Yup, a fella don't know what ta buy these days!" He obviously had no understanding of Dad's theory of economics. Such statements sent us into gales of laughter or fits of silent chuckling, depending on our father's demeanour that evening. Mom, observing Dad try to reply to such a comment, would sometimes dissolve in laughter behind the teapot, wiping tears from her eyes. At other times, when my siblings and I grew too loud, she would ask us about school or other activities, trying to keep the pitch of our voices at a lower than ear-splitting level.

When we had unexpected guests, it became a problem for my mother to make certain items on the menu stretch far enough for everyone. At these times we were quietly advised that the designations "FHB" or "FHI" were to be applied to specified dishes. "FHB" meant "Family Hold Back" while "FHI" stood for "Family Hoe In." Thus, we were often cautioned, "FHI the potatoes, but FHB the dessert."

Inadvertently hilarious things were always happening at our family meals, which quickly dispelled any sense of formality that my mother might have wished to foster. For instance, a huge bowl of mashed potatoes was once flipped onto the floor on its way to the table as its carrier was blindsided by someone gesticulating wildly at the table. One of the hired men, a Polish gentleman who knew very little English, would proudly articulate some swear-word at the table, having no idea of its meaning. At these times, Dad would flush but say nothing, while my brothers and sisters and I looked down and tried not to giggle.

Our dining table was always laid with a white tablecloth, and linen napkins in silver rings were set at each place. These items must have been reminders of an earlier, more genteel lifestyle for Mom, but we children took it all for granted and were mildly surprised at the oilcloths that we saw on the tables of our neighbours.

Against one living-room wall, adjacent to the table, stood a couch that would sag almost to the floor if a few heavy bottoms were planted on it. At night it opened up into a bed with a thin, hard-packed mattress that provided little comfort for the sleeper.

The old cast-iron stove stood majestically apart from the other furniture in the living room. It was a flat-topped, cylindrical stove made to accommodate massive blocks of wood. It was Dad's job to stoke it with huge logs at bedtime so that it glowed cosily throughout the night, and he stirred it into warm, crackling life in the morning. In thirty degrees below weather, I would pull on my underwear in a bedroom (in the winter, any water left standing in a bedroom basin developed a crust of ice overnight), then I'd grab my outer clothes and make a dash for the vicinity of the woodstove. Here the warmth and aroma of the burning logs mingled with the snap and crackle of the pitch on the tamarack as it ignited. It was such a pleasant spot that I would dawdle there and have to be called repeatedly to breakfast.

In another corner stood a battered organ. Though it was badly out of tune, we loved to hear Mom's enthusiastic playing after supper. We would all stand around her and sing discordantly as she played "Big Rock Candy Mountain" or "When the Moon Comes over the Mountain." Any person with a fine ear for music would have been jarred by the off-key renditions we intoned, yet this activity buoyed our spirits and added to a feeling of family togetherness. As there was never money for music lessons, Mom attempted to teach us the rudiments of music, on the old organ. By the time it was my turn to learn, Middle C had ceased to respond to any amount of thumping, making my musical renditions bear little resemblance to the originals.

Recently, I returned to the spot where the homestead had stood, only to find that the house had been bulldozed; all that remained was a decaying heap of lumber, logs and broken glass. As I gazed upon that pile of rubble, a picture of the house as it had been in my youth flashed through my mind, bringing tears to my eyes.

Harvest

Today, as a city dweller, I give little thought to rural life - that is, until fall descends upon us. Then I have only to drive out into the country to remember my past. The sight of the high golden grain against a background of scarlet shrubs and yellow poplars, the pungent aroma of wet leaves and ripe berries, the somnolent warmth of the afternoon sun, and the languorous buzzing of bees all combine to assault my senses with such force that I am transported back to a different time and place.

It was a time when life was undeniably hard but full of rewards. People's lives were close to the earth: they depended on the weather, the rainfall and the soil for their livelihood. Although the outside world impinged upon their lives in the form of prices and quotas, it was nature's whims that were most crucial.

Harvest time was a happy time in our farmhouse, for it was then that the rich return of a summer's work could be reaped. Threshing crews of twelve or fourteen men would work from dawn to dusk, pausing only to eat; they had four meals a day, consuming mountains of food. Food preparation was a major operation, with one or two neighbourhood women helping Mom produce meals that were plentiful and appetizing. Women's reputations as homemakers rested largely on the quality of these offerings.

Mom would get up at four in the morning to set the bread and begin preparing breakfast, which was a hearty meal of porridge followed by bacon, eggs, hash brown potatoes, and big slabs of crusty bread. The men wolfed down their breakfasts and went off to the fields, as the women got down to the serious business of turning out pies and cakes for the day's desserts. A dozen raspberry and blueberry pies, rich red and blue juices oozing from their flaky crusts, would come out of the oven to be swiftly replaced by chocolate and spice cakes. Tantalizing scents filled the house throughout the day. The noon and evening meals consisted of huge roasts of beef or pork with rich brown gravy, or several stuffed chickens, and bowls piled high with fluffy whipped potatoes. Fresh vegetables, such as carrots, beets, beans, and peas, were served with gobs of creamy butter melting over them. The fragrance alone was enough to entrance a small child. I remember Mom's smile at the evident enjoyment and awkward compliments of the men.

I sometimes accompanied her to the field with the afternoon lunches for the threshing crew. We would clatter along through the fields' stubble, the car loaded down with boxes of chicken, ham and egg sandwiches, layer cakes slathered with icing, cream cans filled with lemonade. The men jumped down from their trucks or hayracks to squat on the ground and make short work of lunch. Though they were soon up and back at work, we would linger for a time in the field and savour the ripeness of fall.

I remember sitting on the ground in the mellow afternoon sun one day, absorbing the warmth and inhaling the rich nutty odour of newly threshed grain. I looked up at a big red Massey-Harris threshing machine spewing a rich stream of wheat into a truck box. Another spout sent forth a cloud of fluffy chaff that floated down into a neat, round straw stack. At that moment, I felt that we lived in a sunny realm devoid of threat. A sensation of well-being pervaded my world.

After dark, the men came in from the fields and devoured another feast, then sighed their way off to bed in the bunkhouses. Everyone was exhausted, but Dad's happiness showed in his good humour and twinkling eyes.

"Our crop is good and the price of wheat is up," he whispered to Mom. "It will pay off our debts and see us through the year, with some left over for extras." Though he was generally optimistic, he was jubilant when the harvest was rich. Capricious forces were at work in the perilous occupation of farming, making the rewards of a good harvest all the more valuable.

The memories of those times often fade as I get back into my car and return to the city. Yet, I know that I have only to go out into the country and look out over a wheat field to experience the soft air, to see the carpet of yellow leaves turning brown, to smell the richness around me, and to feel an enveloping sense of optimism once again.

The Choice

In my childhood there were no grandparents, uncles, aunts, or cousins present in my daily life. There were far-off relatives in the eastern Canadian cities, but out in the cold west we were isolated, tossed on a sea of strangers. Our neighbours were interconnected with other families in the district, and we longed to have similar ties of our own

Poverty was the overriding condition in our region: it weighed down on farm families, reducing everyone to a common state of need. Some families were in more impoverished situations than others. We were relatively well off, though we had to watch our pennies, and extra cash was hard to find. Still, we were never near real destitution.

Dad was a very egalitarian man who made no distinction in his mind between himself, with his university education, and our neighbours, some of whom knew only a few words of English. He acknowledged that many of these people, though from different cultures, were just as resourceful as he was, and were probably better farmers.

My siblings and I knew that Dad had one brother who was a lawyer, another who was a medical doctor and a sister who was a writer. Our grandfather had been the founder of Dalhousie Law School in Halifax. We wondered sometimes what had possessed our father to throw his golden opportunities to the winds by choosing the uncertain future of an Alberta farm over a guaranteed affluent lifestyle.

While everyone in our area may have been poor, we never felt deprived ourselves. We had fresh food in abundance and we loved the freedom of the outdoors and the beauty of the land. We had a few things the neighbours lacked, including an organ that Mom played in the evenings, white linen tablecloths on the table (in spite of the back-breaking work of laundering them) and several walls full of books to read.

On our isolated farmstead, we wrapped ourselves in a blanket of pride, though we were told by Mom never to brag to others about our grandfather.

As the years passed, we met a few of our affluent relatives when they descended upon us to pay Dad the respect due to a brother. In their fashionable clothes, they cast pitying glances in our direction from the cushions of their shiny, luxurious cars.

My brothers and sisters and I heard our uncles whispering to Dad one evening.

"Why don't you leave this quagmire of mud and manure and this drab, ramshackle house?" they urged. "You could use your university education to give your children a better life!"

Dad's face clouded and he shook his head. We knew that he did not think that our lives were dark and empty, though he sometimes admitted that poverty may have narrowed our horizons.

"Times will get better," he said, "and the children are healthy and happy on the farm. This is the life I have chosen. I don't think I could make such a big change as you suggest." He ran a hand through his hair and rose from his seat. After silently lighting his lantern, he strode out the front door and into the night. I peered out the window and saw the flickering light swaying back and forth beside his long legs.

When he returned later that night, chores completed, he moved quickly through the living room toward his bedroom door. As he did, one of our uncles looked up from the newspaper he was reading.

"Think about a move and the excitement that could be enjoyed by your children, Robert," he said. Dad said nothing and pushed open the door.

"We'll talk about it later," my uncle said after him.

After overhearing this conversation, we could not help but envision a new and thrilling life. Yet we felt torn: we hoped Dad would be moved by his brothers' pleas, would pluck us up from the farm we knew and deposit us in a bright city where money would flow lavishly into our hands. On the other hand, we loved our father and were hurt by the implied scorn with which the relatives viewed his life, as their derision reflected on us. In the end, when our relatives left, without any commitment from my father to make a change in his lifestyle, we were happy to see them go.

We settled in and enjoyed the outdoors, the community of which we gradually became part and the fun that we created for ourselves. Dad managed to send us all away to get a higher education. We left the farm for greener pastures and brighter lights, keeping a warm spot in our hearts where the memory of our childhood lingered.

As we grew older and moved to various places across Canada and the United States, we came to know some of our cousins who had been raised in affluent city homes, and we learned that their lives had not turned out any better than ours. Today, we no longer envy them, nor do we resent Dad's choice of lifestyle, for we know that our upbringing on the farm has given each of us a strong anchor in the storms of life.

The Streets Run Down to the River

The town of Athabasca is nestled in a snug valley, surrounded by velvety green hills that sweep down to the river. Athabasca is a town animated by both the pioneer era and modern times. Its old, red brick university sits atop a hill like a queen who is surveying her domain. The river flows placidly eastward alongside the town, as it has for centuries. A steel bridge spans it to the north, over which sleek cars now speed. These days, the farmers north of the river have easy access to the amenities and pleasures of the town. This was not the case when I was young.

In its early days, Athabasca was a typical Alberta town. The railroad, a spindly, grey rope of steel, wound its way alongside the river and past towering grain elevators. These elevators, symbols of rural life on the Prairies, stood tall and sturdy, withstanding abuse by wind, dust and frigid Alberta winters.

When I was a child, as we approached the river on our journeys into town, we would sometimes stand at the edge of the hill and look down on Athabasca; it was beautiful in its cozy nook, and seemed to sit there preening and luxuriating in the gifts that nature had bestowed upon it.

To get to the town in those days, we had to cross the river on a rickety ferry that was strung on flimsy cables. It carried six vehicles or six teams of horses with their loads. The air on board smelled of river water, pine needles, rotting wood, manure, horse sweat, and gasoline fumes. Mr. Garten, the ferryman, would jockey the ferry carefully into the landing, and the cars and trucks would rev their motors, spouting smoke as they roared up the hill, while the horses plodded off to the livery stables.

Several steep streets ran perpendicular to the river; on them were cozy houses, churches and schools. The main street, running at an angle away from the ferry landing, provided the necessities of life. Its many stores showed off attractive wares in their display windows. On the corner near the river stood the Grand

Union Hotel, which was down at heel even when I was young. Through the open doors of the beer parlour there spewed the odours of onion soup and beer, and the sound of loud voices. I always passed this den of vice as fast as I could because I sensed that untold evils lurked within.

Across the street stood the Royal Café, run by a Chinese gentleman named Charlie. (Nobody seemed to know his surname or even wonder if he had one.) Above this café hung a huge pink ice-cream cone that never ceased to tickle my senses in anticipation of a sweet dessert. The café had green wooden booths that could each hold six people. As I grew older, I would sometimes hang out there with other teenagers, eating raisin pie and watching truck drivers flirt with the waitresses.

Near the hotel was Mike's Dry Goods Store. I loved to shop there because it held a little bit of everything. A person could buy rubber boots, ladies' straw hats, overalls, Mackinaw jackets, nylon stockings, bras, lace panties, sober navy blue suits for gentlemen, and frothy party dresses, anything one's heart desired.

A little farther along the street stood the drugstore, erect and proper with the sober, grey-suited Mr. Cull presiding within. A customer had to stand at his counter and request the needed items; then Mr. Cull would collect them, wrap them in brown paper and present them formally to the buyer. When a woman wanted to buy sanitary napkins, she would have to "case" the store in the hope of finding a female clerk on duty, for Mr. Cull was altogether too intimidating.

Across from the drugstore was the squat red brick telephone office. Sim Lewis sat in a swivel chair all day, taking calls and joking with everyone who called. He was replaced in the evenings by his daughters, Chick, Velma, and Shirley - the most beautiful girls north of Hollywood, with radiant smiles and lovely, liquid brown eyes - who sat in the office wearing their earphones and directing calls. As the calls came in, they plugged cords into the holes that represented individual homes and businesses. When a long distance call came in from out of town, they always answered with "Athabasc." We never knew why, but it seemed to be a sort of international code for our town. Behind the office was the family's living quarters, from which one could often hear the girls' carefree laughter. It was a happy place that many young people loved to visit.

A little farther up the hill, on the same side of the street, stood Parkers' General Store. The most interesting thing about this store was the movie theatre and dance hall above it. On Saturday afternoons we climbed the rickety stairs and slipped into this musty, darkened space; we felt our way between the folding chairs as black and white images flashed jerkily by on the screen. On special Saturday nights the theatre became a dancehall. Most of the chairs were moved out, save for the few that were set along the wall for old folks and those girls not chosen to dance. The floor was made slippery by a sprinkling of green waxy flakes, allowing dancers to twirl and glide gracefully across its surface. Many a romance had blossomed on this dance floor.

Past Parkers' Store was the imposing Imperial Bank of Canada. Dignified, sturdy white pillars framed its front door. It was quiet and stuffy inside, with a wall separating the bank officials from the shabby farmers and the merchants in their shiny suits. Two tellers peered out at customers from behind thin metal bars, taking in cheques and sliding out money.

On the corner of the next street was Hingley's Tannery. Here the hides of such animals as mink, rabbit, fox, marten, raccoon, and beaver were hung from the ceiling on stretching frames to dry. The stench coming from this building was enough to make a person want to sprint by at top speed.

At a little distance from this tannery stood Falconer's Hardware Store, showing off its fine Blue Willow china and beautiful blue-eyed dolls in the windows. As a child, I longed to touch the dolls' shiny curls; when I was older, I wished instead for some of the lovely crystal stemware. In Falconer's, the pungent odour of the dark oiled floor mingled with the smell of kerosene; as farm-

44

ers filled cans with the fuel for their lamps and lanterns, some of it spilled off and seeped into the floorboard cracks. These scents, though strong, were comfortingly familiar, and they failed to mar the delicate touch created by the elegant china and glassware.

On this same street was Redden's Grocery Store. The aromas of all kinds of foods would tease my nostrils as I passed. There were big wheels of sharp cheddar cheese; there were open bins of nuts, candy and ginger snaps waiting to be scooped into bags and taken to the counter to be priced; and there were wooden boxes of apples and oranges, and clumps of bananas dangling from hooks on the ceiling. Handsome young boys whistled as they filled cardboard boxes and smiled at the customers as they carried the groceries to cars or trucks.

Toward the top of these streets stood narrow two-storey houses with wide verandas where people would sit in their porch swings in the evening. At the very top of the hill was the red school where I learned mathematics, literature and chemistry - and the art of flirting with boys.

It was in Athabasca that I spent my teenage years. It was there that I careened down the hill on my bicycle and plodded laboriously up it; it was there that I learned to dance; it was there that I received my first kiss; it was there that I grew up. This town, so similar in structure to many other small Alberta towns, was unique and special to me. In the bustling Athabasca of today, if I listen, I can hear the hills whisper tales of that time.

The Pink Slip

Mom was sitting at the dining table with an Eaton's catalogue and a store order form spread out before her. She had already ordered a few household necessities: new towels to replace the thin, hole-ridden ones hanging by the washbasin, and an aluminium saucepan to take the place of the battered pot that continued to leak no matter how many times it was mended with solder. She looked happy, clutching a few dollar bills tightly in her hand as she gazed at the brightly coloured pictures on the catalogue pages. What else is she sending for, I wondered, as I peered over her shoulder.

To my surprise, the catalogue was open to the lingerie pages. There were corsets and garter belts, bloomers and scanty lace panties, modern brassieres, and a lovely pink satin slip. I could see that her eyes were focused on the latter. She usually wore cotton slips made from bleached flour sacks, with wide straps sewn solidly to the bodice. Now I realize that she might have felt such bulky undergarments made her look frumpy; but I was young then, I took her for granted and paid little attention to her appearance. Yet even I could not help but notice her happy flush as she sat looking at the catalogue, and I imagined how pretty she would look with a slim slip under her graceful blue dress.

"What are you sending for?" I asked.

"This," she said, smiling, pointing at the shimmering and thin-strapped slip. "I've saved my money for several months, and now I have five dollars. I'm ordering this slip for myself."

I hugged her, enjoying the pleasant glow on her cheeks, and watched as she filled in the rest of the order and folded five one-dollar bills into the envelope to be sent off to the Eaton's in Winnipeg. She tucked the envelope in beside the red china hen that sat on the sideboard and gazed at it with satisfaction.

"Can't you just see me swirling around at the box social, with my blue crêpe dress clinging nicely to me over this lovely

46

slip?" Box socials were lively fundraising events in our community. Each woman or girl attending it would take a colourfully wrapped boxed lunch, then the boxes were auctioned off to the men in the audience. The woman or girl would then have lunch with the man who had bought her box. Mom loved to go to these lunches. Although she laughed at the idea of "dressing up" in her pink slip for the next one, I knew that she was anticipating a rare opportunity to look smart and elegant. It had been such a long time since she had worn pretty clothes that she probably forgot what it felt like.

She stepped into the kitchen and began to peel potatoes and prepare the other vegetables for dinner. A loud rapping on the door interrupted our peaceful mood.

"Answer the door, dear," she said. "It's probably a neighbour stopping for a cup of tea." I opened the door to find a man clad in several layers of tattered clothes that were bound together by safety pins and shoelaces. His hair was a dirty blond colour, long and straggly, and his chin was covered with a few weeks' worth of stubble. His cheeks were hollow and none too clean.

"May I speak with your mother?" he asked in a soft, rather pleasant voice.

"Yes," I answered, preferring that Mom dealt with him. I beckoned to her to come to the door.

"Hello!" she said and smiled at the unkempt wayfarer as she wiped her hands on her apron. "Can I do something for you?"

"You certainly can, if you're kind enough," he answered. "I'm terribly hungry. I haven't had anything to eat in three days. Can I do some chores or split some wood for you to earn a meal?" he asked. "Please?" he added, seeming to sense that politeness would further his cause. His offer appeared to be an honest proposition, and his words were clear and well articulated.

"Of course you can. But before you start, please sit down on the step for a while and rest while I make you some sandwiches." The scruffy wanderer sat down, his Adam's apple bobbing up and down in anticipation of the promised food. Poor fellow, I thought. It must be awful to have no home and no food.

Mom laid a place for him on the table and set out two thick bologna sandwiches and a bowl of her homemade tomato soup. His skinny jaws jiggled and his dark eyes glistened as he took his seat. Unable to wait a minute longer, he snatched one sandwich with his grubby fist and devoured it greedily as if it was the last food he would ever have. He took a little more time with the second sandwich, chewing it carefully. He slurped the first part of his soup eagerly, letting it dribble down his whiskered chin; then he ate it more slowly, wiping his mouth with the napkin my mother had placed beside him. It was evident that he could remember better times.

Mom sat across the table from him and asked, "How did you get into such a desperate predicament?" It was the time of the Depression, and poverty had enveloped the country. Fortunately, my family had plenty of food. Every now and then a tramp would wander our way, asking for assistance. Mom wanted to hear this one's story.

"Well, Ma'am, I've fallen on hard times. I'm homeless and most of the time I'm hungry. I lost my job in Windsor, Ontario, when the Ford factory laid off most of its workers. I couldn't find another job, and my wife moved out because I couldn't afford to buy food or pay the rent. She took our two children and settled with her parents. I couldn't hang around there sponging off them, so I rode the rails toward B.C., hoping to find a job. What a foolish dream that was! Now I sleep in barns and haystacks most nights. It's cold and lonely, and I haven't heard from my wife since I left Ontario. I don't have her address, so I can't write to her even if she wanted to hear from me."

He sniffed away the tears that had been brimming in his eyes. "Thank you, Ma'am," he said, "you're very kind. I'll chop your wood now." He went outside and swung our axe energetically, splitting round blocks of wood into small pieces for our kitchen range. When he had finished chopping the pile, he came to the door and thanked Mom once again.

"I'll be going now," he said. "I'm heading back to town and then I'll try to ride the rails to Vancouver. I can ride in a boxcar when the train is moving, but when the train stops, I have to cling to the bottom of a car. If nobody finds me there, I'll be very lucky. I have relatives on the coast of British Columbia and they'll help me if I make it there. I might even find a job."

"Here," Mom said as she handed him a brown paper bag. Inside it was a loaf of bread and a large chunk of cheddar cheese. I could see, as he smiled at her, that there was a nice man living under the many layers of rags and whiskers.

"Wait a minute," Mom said quickly as he turned to leave. I wondered what other food she would bestow upon him. She went to the sideboard and picked up the envelope she had prepared to send to Eaton's. She plucked out the five one-dollar bills and folded them into a small wad that she thrust into his callused hand.

"I hope you make it to Vancouver," she said.

He smiled at her again, showing nice, even teeth. "Thank you, Ma'am. You are a real, true Christian. If I'm ever rich, I'll return this money to you." Then he turned and headed down the road to town.

Mom watched him through the window as he strode away.

"Doesn't he look ravishing in my satin slip?" she asked with a chuckle. I stood beside her and looked out the window. I imagined him sashaying along with the pink slip swirling around his knees, with his ragged dirt-encrusted pants sticking out below. Mom and I shared a smile. To this day I can still visualize that tramp in a shimmering pink slip marching down the rutted country road.

A Gentle Heart

Because our mother passed away when I was young, some of my memories of her are sharp and clear, while others float in forgotten times.

Our father was a gentle man who ran the farm as best he could. At a time when most men ruled their families and made all the decisions, he left the raising of the family to Mom. He was aware of her wisdom and her strength; indeed, she was the glue that held the family together, and our anchor in the world.

When I was small, she was my life. She had endless patience and tolerance and rarely became disturbed or angry. If mishaps occurred, or if chaos reigned over the household, she met it all with humour. Although she was busy with the endless tasks that kept a farm functioning, she still found time to read to me, to prepare my favourite dishes, to sew attractive clothes for me, to give me advice on school assignments, and to let me help her in simple chores. I was wrapped in a blanket of her love that protected me from all harm.

I remember the warmth of her body as she lay beside me on my narrow cot at bedtime, bringing tears to my eyes with her readings of *The Elephant's Child* or *Oliver Twist*. I remember the exciting stories she made up for me as she rocked back and forth in her old rocking chair until she nodded off and whatever sewing she had been working on slipped to the floor.

I remember the relaxed relationship we shared as I kneaded her bread dough and sifted coloured decorations onto cookies, or as we sat outside together in the afternoon sun pulling husks off ears of corn in preparation for supper. I remember she was tired in the evenings from the daily toil, yet her humour always prevailed and preserved her. She often told us about going to bed so exhausted that she thought she might be ill the next morning; then she would admit with a rueful smile that, in spite of this prediction, she usually awoke feeling fine.

I remember her laughter in the face of mishaps that could have defeated her. I once helped her chase and corner a rooster that was meant to provide Sunday dinner for the minister. He had arrived with his family at our house rather unexpectedly one afternoon. As they waited with anticipation in the living room, Mom and I pursued the fleeing bird. He squawked indignantly as he raced around the hen yard, eluding our grasp. We finally managed to trap him. Since Dad was working in the fields (a deliberate evasion that we didn't even try to explain to the minister), we were confronted with the task of converting a rebellious live chicken into a nicely browned, stuffed main course for Sunday dinner.

But, the rooster had other ideas. He thrashed around and flapped his wings as I held his feet and Mom tried to decapitate him. She raised an axe menacingly into the air while I tried to keep him on the chopping block. He eyed us with resentment. She couldn't bring the axe down on him. She dropped it and grabbed him resolutely by the neck - she would strangle him instead! She twisted and pulled on his stringy, elastic neck, but he only squawked and looked balefully at us. Eventually, she gave up the struggle and let him go. He fluffed out his feathers and strutted off regally, much offended by his treatment, while we collapsed on the ground and laughed until we cried.

Mom went inside and prepared a dinner of vegetables and an omelette that she formally presented to the minister and his family. He harrumphed disapprovingly, though he did help himself to a generous portion.

The False Promise

An old black mantel clock chimed out the hours of my childhood; it was the rhythm of my days and nights. In the early days, the loud and echoing "ding-dong" that reverberated periodically through the night never disturbed my sleep. Rather, it was a reassuring sort of sound: faintly melancholy, but dependable. It provided a comforting continuum for a small child. Our house was always bustling with varied activities, and it might have given way to chaos but for this steady tolling of the hours. As long as this clock ordered our days, my life was safe and predictable.

Then our mother was gone, and my world fell apart. Suddenly, the notes that the clock jangled out were discordant and harsh. I ceased to revere it, feeling that its message of comfort had been a sham and its promise of continuity false. For all these years, I thought, my steadfast old clock has been chiming out a hypocritical message. I could count on nothing.

Only now, in my later life, am I able to hear a clock strike the hours without a feeling of betrayal.

Lonely Walk

I was feeling sorry for myself as I wandered around in the dark and chilly house. Outside, bright sunlight glinted off the melting snow, and the world seemed warm and fresh. Inside, Saturday and Sunday loomed drearily ahead of me.

It had been a difficult year for me. Mom's sister had come to stay at the farmhouse to care for me after Mom's death, but the sadness that had enveloped my life at that time made me sulky and rebellious. My aunt and I had endured each other for only a few months. She came from Texas and had such a Southern drawl that I often did not comprehend what she was saying. One day, my friend Helen dropped in on her way home from school. Aunt Bessie asked us to go outside and pick some "pissy willows" to put on the dining-room table. Helen laughed until she cried, and told all the other pupils at school. I had been so embarrassed: it had taken me forever to live down that event.

After Aunt Bessie left, my sister Nan came home to care for me; it was a very generous gesture, for she had given up her school year in the city to do so. I adored and idolized her. Then she, too, had left, to attend a three-week course in town, and I was alone with Dad.

As I wandered around the house, a wonderful idea that had been simmering in my mind suddenly bubbled up and propelled me into action. I rushed outside looking for Dad, and found him in the warm cow barn. His cheek was nestled against a cow's flank and his hands squeezed thin streams of milk rhythmically into a tin pail. I sidled up to him.

"Daddy, can we go to town today?" I begged. "I want to see Nan. She's been gone two weeks now and she said I could visit her in town. Please, can we go?"

"Don't be silly, dear," he answered curtly. "Of course we can't! I have too much work to do and besides, the car is out of commission. Couldn't you just read a book?"

"If I can't get a drive, may I ride my bike to town?" I asked, hoping to find an acceptable alternative.

"Through all this slush and mud? I wouldn't try it!"

"May I walk to town?" I pleaded, growing desperate. "Ten miles isn't so far! It's only nine o'clock, and if I start out now I'll be there by noon. Nan really wanted me to call on her in town. Please, Daddy," I implored.

He stood up, milk pail in hand. "Well, if you're brave enough for that, go ahead," he said, looking me straight in the eye. I didn't flinch. Now I had to do it. I had turned eleven and I needed to show my independence. "But wear your snowsuit and phone me if Nan wants you to stay overnight," he called after me as I sped toward the house.

I rushed inside, put on my snowsuit, and brushed my hair until it shone. I had washed it the night before just in case we went into town. Nan always said I had pretty hair, and I wanted her to be proud of me when she introduced me to her friends.

I set off into the bright day, almost blinded by the sun sparkling off the snow. A few cars passed me, their passengers waving hello, but no one offered me a ride. I didn't mind, for the day was glorious, and I revelled in thoughts of how surprised and pleased Nan would be to see me. I reached town about noon, and though I was hot, sweaty and hungry, I decided to find Nan right away. Maybe she would buy me some lunch. I headed quickly for the street where the youth hostel she was staying in was located. I could hardly wait to see her joyous reaction.

I spied a car out in front of her building as I drew near. Six young people were hooting with laughter as they piled inside it, one on top of another. I spotted Nan among them, so I waved and shouted. She must be going downtown, and I knew she wouldn't want to miss me. She got out of the car and walked slowly toward me. She wasn't smiling and didn't look pleased.

"How did you get here?" she demanded, obviously annoyed.

"I walked," I answered proudly, with a big smile.

Nan looked distressed. This was not the reception I had expected. She suddenly smiled and patted my shoulder. "Oh, honey," she said in her sweetest voice, "I'm sorry, but we're all going out to the Woods' farm. This is their car, and we've been invited for lunch, you see, so I have to go! You don't mind, do you?" When I didn't answer, she went on. "Here's twenty-five cents. You can buy yourself a hamburger at the Royal Café, and I'm sure there'll be someone around to give you a ride back. I'll be home in a week. See you!" With that, she climbed into the car and planted herself on someone's knee. Muddy water and gravel sprayed up at me from the spinning wheels as the car drove off. I waved, though no one seemed to notice.

Determined not to cry, I plodded down the hill to the café where I bought a hamburger. I ate it in a green booth, while I watched a pretty waitress in a green uniform flirt with a bus driver. I bought a chocolate bar, which would break into ten pieces, one for each mile that I had to walk home.

I trudged along the road home through the long afternoon. As the sun dropped down to the horizon, a damp chill settled in. A few cars passed me on the road, crammed with people and groceries; no one stopped for me. When I finally arrived home, my father had the lamps lit against the falling dusk. He was preparing his version of a meal: fried potatoes and scrambled eggs. It sent off a warm, buttery aroma, and the helping he prepared for me tasted wonderful. He asked no questions, but came around the table and gave me one of his rare pats on my back.

When Nan's course was over, she brought home a white baseball cap as a present for me. She cleaned up the house, cooked my favourite foods, and was ever so nice to me. My failed visit to town made me realize I was not the centre of anyone else's universe. This knowledge has lingered in my mind throughout my life, quelling any of my more unrealistic expectations.

A Space to Cross

Dad's wide straw hat cast a shadow over his features. Because it was Sunday, he was wearing his second-best clothes on his tall and sinewy frame. He strode along purposefully, occasionally stopping to wait for me to catch up to him. I was wearing rolled-up jeans and a blue shirt. My hair was escaping from a blue ribbon, and he ruffled it tentatively when I caught up to him. I did not let myself react.

I walked beside him down to a narrow furrow in the wheat field. The wheat stocks thrust themselves up between us symbolically. He broke off some kernels in his hand, rubbing away the chaff, and gave them to me to eat. They were gummy, tasting of nuts. He said that they were almost ripe and ready to thresh. Threshing time was always an exciting time on the farm, yielding both wonderful food and the promise of extra money to spend. I nodded in response to his comment without much enthusiasm.

Our mother was gone. Thoughts of her death consumed me. Dad took me along with him to many different places around the neighbourhood, trying in his way to communicate with me. I knew this in my heart, so I went along with him when he invited me. Yet I could not forgive him for his aloofness. I felt that he was not as warm and loving as Mom had been.

We wandered back through the barnyard and stopped at the corral. A small sorrel pony came galloping up and reached out to nuzzle him. He patted her nose and asked, "Would you like to try riding Jill? I can saddle her up for you."

"No, thanks," I replied. "I'd rather ride my bike."

"Well, then," he said, "let's feed her some oats. I think she deserves a treat. I'll get a pail."

"Okay," I answered. When he came back with the oats, I stood aside while the horse snorted up the offering. Satisfied, the little pony flicked her tail and romped away. Dad and I wandered back to the house. He made tea for himself and offered me milk and some of the cookies the hired girl had made. I drank the milk, but only nibbled at a cookie. It tasted like glue and stuck in my throat. Why couldn't that girl try some of Mom's recipes? Then I picked up my book, and Dad went back to his newspaper. Silence enveloped us.

After a time, he tried again to cross the chasm between us.

"Did you know that the Allies have established another beachhead in North Africa?" he asked, laying aside his paper.

"Oh? What's a beachhead?" I asked.

He explained that a beachhead was a sort of base established on the coast by landing troops; he said that the news might be a sign of the beginning of the end of the War. He sounded optimistic. I listened to him then because I was worried about my brother, who was at sea, and my cousin, who was flying bombers over Germany. I did hope the war would soon be over.

"Do you know why the price of wheat goes up and down?" he asked, shifting to another topic in an attempt to engage me in a new conversation.

"No," I answered. As he tried to explain, I tuned him out. He's always going on as if he's giving a classroom lecture, I thought. We retreated again into our separate worlds.

If only he had been able to bend a little more, perhaps we could have come closer together. If only I had said, "Yes, I'd love to go riding!" when he had asked, then I would have seen his eyes glow with pleasure. If only he had been able to reach out and touch me, the love that lay smothered under his layers of manners would have blossomed and flourished. If only I had listened more to his "lectures," I would have been way ahead of my teachers. If only he had been able to talk with me about girl things - friends who turned against me, what to do with my hair - he could have filled the void in my life. If only I had thrown my arms around his neck and said, "I love you." He would have pretended to be embarrassed; really, he would have been filled with joy.

57

If only! I was thirteen years old, having reached the stage where I had to assert my independence, and would not display love to anyone in authority. So we sat in the echoing room, he with the *Manchester Guardian* and I with *Anne of Green Gables,* and we failed to touch. Only later, when I was grown and he was gone, did I know the strength of our love. I feel sure that he had always known it.

The town of Athabasca, c. 1940

The river at Athabasca, early 1940's

The Athabasca River cage
1933

Athabasca River and the ferry, early 1930's

FERRY AT ATHABASCA

The Farmhouse, c. 1931

The Weldon family: George, Dad, Audrey (baby), Mom, Margaret, Ralph and Nan

The threshing gang, c. 1933

Audrey's father, c. 1948

Audrey in the field
age 3

Audrey, age 5, and her dog, Brick

Audrey on the swing, age 9

Audrey in front of the farmhouse
age 12

Margaret and Audrey, 1939

Audrey's high school in Athabasca

Audrey, age 15, playing hookey
with her friends

Audrey and Jack on their Honeymoon
1951

Audrey and Jack's little daughter, Donna
age 3

The Reid Family (Carol, Jack, Audrey and Rob) 2002

Double Exposure

In my mind, I am revisiting my father's house. I drive up a red brick driveway that is set between stately elms. I get out of my car and walk up a sidewalk bordered with geraniums, petunias and alyssum that cuts through a lush, well-tended lawn. The sweet aroma of lilacs and roses draws me on, up to the door, and I bang the big brass knocker.

I stand resolutely at the door until it is answered, awaiting my father as I wish him to be. A housekeeper responds to my knock and I am led quietly over a deep burgundy carpet to his book-lined study. Wearing a vested suit with a watch chain, he rises from behind his massive oak desk and puts down the gold pen with which he has been writing. He smiles and holds out his arms to me. His blue eyes crinkle, and his face glows with pleasure.

Overlaid on this fantasy scene like a double exposure is another picture that refuses to fade and disappear - the picture of truth. In this second scene, the driveway is a rutted dirt track, and the wooden walkway to the house is bordered with hard-packed earth and chickweed. Hops and scarlet runner beans obscure the weathered walls of the house, and only a dilapidated screen door, hanging aslant, stands sentinel over the family home. Earthy smells surround me: new-mown hay, fresh and frothy milk, horse sweat, and cow manure.

Inside, Dad sits at the battered oak dining table, scribbling in a pad with a stubby pencil that he moistens now and then with his tongue. It is his stolen hour at day's end when he can add a few lines to his memoirs. He is wearing a tattered work shirt and bib overalls that are stained with loam from the fields. His thin, weather-beaten face is tense with concentration, though when he looks up his deep blue eyes crinkle merrily.

I push this image aside and go on determinedly with the picture that I want to create. The family is seated around the dining-room table. A place is reserved for me, and I join them. The table is set with snowy linen, fine china and silver serving dishes. A crystal chandelier glitters above us. Yet it is casting an incongruous, glaring white light.

Suddenly, I see the stark white mantles of a gas lamp and I hear the hiss of gas under pressure. The immaculate tablecloth is now stained where the black elbows of hired hands have deposited little heaps of chaff and earth. The decorum is shattered by boisterous laughter and strident voices vying for attention.

I push aside this insistent second scene once again and focus on my dream picture. From the grand piano in the living room there emanates the soft notes of classical music. A stately woman sits at the piano, her pale, manicured hands skating up and down the keyboard. It is my mother, and she is beautiful.

Then in the shadows I see Mom in her faded housedress, thumping the chipped keys of our wheezing organ as she tries to play "Happy Days Are Here Again."

Once more, I force this image to become transparent. I see my father rise and stand by the glowing fire in the fireplace. He launches enthusiastically into one of his little "talks," expounding on one or two political systems - this time, conservatism and democratic socialism - then he changes gears and is off on a lecture about symbolism in T.S. Eliot's "The Hollow Men."

Another scene stubbornly takes form and superimposes itself over this picture. In this picture of the real past, Dad is sitting at the end of the battered table, tilting back his hard wooden chair, while discussing exactly the same subjects.

My two pictures converge; my wish image fades and floats away. Given the chance, I would have created an easier, more gracious lifestyle for my father, as I felt he had deserved. Yet the gentle man with the crinkly blue eyes remains constant in these two images. In his tattered work clothes, holding his stubby pencil, he was better than I ever could have dreamed.

60

The Tea Party

I was recently a guest at an afternoon tea party. Dainty sandwiches were served to accompany the tea, which was ceremoniously dispensed from a silver service into delicate china cups. In the midst of the subdued conversation, I found myself recalling an event of my youth.

There was a very proper matron who lived in Athabasca, out on the edge of the town. Mrs. Fell was the undisputed social leader of the community, and to receive an invitation to tea at her prestigious residence was the ultimate social honour. Once, I was included in an invitation that had been given to my sister; as a teacher, Margaret was allowed into this select society on rare occasions. The appointed afternoon arrived and, dressed in our best but most conservative clothes, we ventured forth into Athabasca's high society.

Mrs. Fell's house was huge; in my naive judgment, I also thought it to be richly appointed. It had heavily patterned carpets, sombre wallpaper, dark woodwork, and overstuffed furniture. Stern family portraits glowered from the walls; beautiful blue and white china plates rested in their wall brackets and added a touch of delicacy to the austere rooms.

We were greeted with formal handshakes at the door and then politely conducted into the parlour. We recognized friends and neighbours among the guests who were already seated in the parlour, and they appeared to be equally cowed by the grandeur of their surroundings. Tea was duly served in beautiful Belleek cups, and muted conversation ensued. All of us were taking our cues for behaviour from the regal dowager who was our hostess. My hands trembled from fear of spilling something or committing some other unforgivably gauche act.

Suddenly, in the midst of all the ceremony, someone broke wind! The abrupt noise seemed to bounce around the room and

61

ricochet off the walls, before settling down with a resonating "f-t, f-f-t, f-f-f-t." My cheeks burned with embarrassment. When I dared to raise my eyes, I perceived that all of the proper ladies of the town were shaking with soundless laughter, their tea splashing back and forth in their cups. Later, as the guests left Mrs. Fell's sombre residence, unrestrained laughter could be heard along the road to town.

From that time on, whenever Marg and I met the people who had been at that tea, we made sure to smile and wave, or stop to talk. Mrs. Fell still walked with her head held high, but she no longer intimidated us. Her tea party became known around town as the "fart party," and from then on she was an ordinary citizen who engendered smiles from the townspeople.

Burnt Chicken

When I was small, I often declared that I wanted to be just like Peggy when I grew up. Peggy was our family's affectionate nickname for my sister Marg. While I have never managed to achieve this goal (unfortunately, not being gifted with her serene good nature) I have never ceased to try. My earliest, clearest memories of Marg recall her warm hugs and the exciting stories she would tell when she arrived home on holiday from high school or normal school.

Following close on the heels of her relaxed greetings were her furious cleaning bouts. She would look around with dismay at the disorder that characterized our home and attack it with zeal, somehow managing to get most of the family members enthusiastically involved in the cleanup. The barnyard was in close proximity to the house, so straw, chaff, mud, and other "delicacies" were trailed in with every person who entered. Marg couldn't rest until all rooms were clean and tidy.

I was usually put to dusting and had to ferret out every particle of dust lurking in the curlicues on the legs of the oak dining table, the organ and its stool, and the intricate woodwork on the sideboard. My other contribution was to hold my legs and arms stiff while both my sisters pushed me back and forth, polishing the newly waxed linoleum floor with my bottom.

At other times, Marg would decide to plaster yet another sheet of wallpaper on the walls. The dining table became a platform on which we laid the paper and slathered it with a paste of flour and water; then we would slap the wallpaper onto the walls with little regard for angle or symmetry. The main thing was to cover up the dark marks on the ceiling where the rain had found its way through the roof.

When all was to her satisfaction, she would settle in and entertain us with stories of her adventures in normal school or in her teaching positions. These stories held me enthralled: I still remember the names of her friends better than those of mine. Later, we would do other fun things, like making shortbread and fudge, or going for a swim in the river. The next time she came home she would find dirt and disorder again, and the whole process would be repeated.

When I reached the ninth grade and could no longer attend our country school, Marg applied for a teaching position in Athabasca; though this action was for the sole purpose of meeting my needs, I didn't know or appreciate it at the time. However, she certainly gained a bonus from this move, as my teacher was Bill Clow, the man who would later become her husband, and, several years on, a mover and shaker in the oil industry. It wasn't long before he was a regular visitor in the little apartment Marg and I had taken together in Athabasca. With his wonderful sense of humour, he had us both quaking with laughter many a time.

When I look back now, I realize that undertaking the care, nurturing and guidance of a fourteen-year-old in a new and exciting environment must have been a daunting task for my sister. I had just become interested in the opposite sex, and was seeing my first boyfriend. Perhaps the fact that I was venturing into the teenage world was a concern for my sister, but she never seemed disturbed by the attentions of this boy and always seemed to trust me. I never felt that I was a worry for Margaret. Her good nature and sense of fun prevailed, and two years went by in a flurry of activity and high spirits.

Only once did I arouse her anger. On that occasion, the problem, predictably, concerned me forsaking my share of the cleaning. Our family was rather permissive about sleeping late in the morning, and anyone who was tired thought nothing of staying in bed until noon. One Saturday, I carried this laid-back attitude a little too far.

Marg had left me in our apartment and gone on a shopping trip to Edmonton. This involved catching a bus from Athabasca at seven in the morning, journeying three hours to the city, shopping for six or seven hours, and returning at eight in the evening. The tasks she had asked me to complete during her absence included finishing my homework, going grocery shopping, doing the washing, and cleaning the apartment. Of course, Marg required every inch of that tiny apartment to gleam and sparkle - at least, as far as its rather dingy nature would permit.

Marg arrived home after her long and exhausting day, and was gripped by panic when her astonished gaze lit on a basket of dirty laundry, and a table littered with breakfast dishes, spilled milk and an array of cereal boxes. She was struck with the fear that I had been abducted, or that some other terrible fate had befallen me. When she rushed into the bedroom and found me contentedly napping, she was understandably perturbed. I remember scrambling out of bed, doing the cleaning as fast as I could, and washing clothes far into the night in an effort to mollify her and restore her usual good humour. Later that evening she asked me dryly, "Audrey, did you have a nice day?"

Our little apartment was a two-room affair in the back yard of Mr. Daigneau's house. The apartment, his house and a row of sheds together formed a "U" around his backyard, enclosing his garden. If we stepped off the sidewalk in front of our door, we stepped directly into his onion patch. In general, this arrangement did not bother us, but when he spread a thick layer of pungent manure on the soil, the buildings trapped the aroma and our little domain was permeated with an acrid stench. During such times, we abruptly curtailed our entertaining and spent as little time as possible at home until the smell dissipated.

Another memory I have of those years with Marg also involves a strong odour. Often we would leave a pot of stew or some other concoction simmering on the back of the woodstove during the day, and we would stir up the fire and finish cooking it after school. One day, a pot of chicken was left on the hottest part of the stove and the fire was stoked up to burn until noon. I do not doubt that this oversight was mine.

65

As I walked home from school for lunch, a journey of less than a block, a strange smell began to assail my nostrils. When I came to Mr. Daigneau's backyard, its source was apparent. Marg, also on her lunch break, arrived at the same moment and together we opened our door to a cloud of thick black smoke. An overwhelming stench of burnt chicken poured forth to flood the neighbourhood. People paused on their way past our building to wonder about the origin of the terrible smell. The pot with the chicken in it was severely damaged: the chicken was black and fossilized, permanently welded to the sides of the charred vessel. We pitched the whole thing outdoors where it continued to emit its fumes and attract comments from passersby.

When I returned to school in the afternoon, I noticed my classmates looking at me oddly and moving away. I ran home at recess to change my clothes, but found that everything hanging in the closet was redolent of burnt chicken. Marg arrived at the same time to change her clothes, for even her adoring first graders had exclaimed, "Gee, Miss Weldon, you smell funny!"

That evening we hung all our clothes outside to air. Although we scoured that little apartment's every nook and cranny and sprayed air freshener generously around, the acrid smell lingered for weeks. The memory of it still makes my eyes burn. If this incident was due to my carelessness, blame was never attributed to me: it simply fell into the annals of family lore.

Those two years in Athabasca were probably my happiest as I was growing up. Marg and I enjoyed each other's company, and in striving for her approval, I became a good deal tidier and more concerned with cleanliness. Her sweet nature and her wonderful sense of humour have never changed. She has always been the person upon whom I have modelled my life.

My Sister Beside Me

My sister Nan was sensitive and easily moved. Every sad story, true or not, that generated small sighs from other people, would cause her to burst forth in a torrent of tears. Her emotions always lurked just under the surface, ready to emerge as either laughter or deep distress. Whenever she heard some doleful tale about a person she barely knew, she displayed great empathy.

I was her little sister, pampered and indulged by her. If I was disappointed in anything, she would console me or find an activity to restore my happiness. When I started school and received several smacks with the strap on my very first day, she tried to defend me to the teacher. She dared to stand up for me many times at school, and for these efforts she was purposely ignored and left to glean her education out of books with little help from anyone at school. Once, the teacher, annoyed as she often was by Nan's defence of me, recommended that my sister quit school and scrub floors for a living. In spite of this prediction, Nan attained a much better education than that of the miserable teacher, and never scrubbed anyone's floor but her own.

Nan loved to sew and often made nicer outfits for me than anything that could be ordered from the Eaton's catalogue. These creations were so pretty that they were to be worn only on festive occasions. I remember rushing home from school on one of my birthdays, absolutely certain that Nan had made a lovely new outfit for me. Sure enough, one was hanging in the middle of the living room for all to see. I was delighted!

Whenever our sister Margaret went to a dance or out to dinner, Nan made her a fashionable new outfit. This tactic backfired once, and Nan could only laugh at the result. A young man named Allen Baskerville invited Marg out to dinner one Sunday evening. Assuming that he had a car and would take Marg to town, Nan made a beautiful blue dress for the event. To our chagrin, he arrived on a big, rawboned white horse and informed us that he was taking Marg to dinner at a neighbour's house, where he worked as a hired hand. Margaret, in her frilly dress, realized that it was too late to change into slacks; so off she went, seated behind the young man, her dress flipping up in the wind on both sides. We giggled as we watched her flutter off down the road.

Nan loved to dance and would glide around the hall with any boy who invited her to join him in a polka, foxtrot or waltz. She would cajole and beg our brothers to take her to any dance being held in the local community halls. George and Ralph loved her dearly and were easily persuaded to take her wherever she wanted to go. They would set off together in an old car, on horseback or in a sleigh and return home happily in the small hours of the morning.

Once, Nan was determined to go to a particular dance, though there was no car or saddle horse available to transport her for the evening. After making several suggestions for alternative means of transportation and failing to get my father's approval, she grew desperate.

"Well, how about taking Bess and the drag?" she asked innocently. Our family responded with much laughter. Bess was a bulky workhorse, and the "drag" was a stone-boat only used to haul water and stones. In the face of everyone's laughter, she finally gave up.

Whatever Nan decided to do, she did with all her heart. She loved all the animals on the farm and had a personal relationship with each cow, horse, dog, and cat - and perhaps each pig, as well. She knew each animal's individual characteristics, and she knew exactly how to get around their foibles. She would ride the fastest horses we had and challenge our brothers to races. She didn't always win, but she rode like a true jockey, standing high in the stirrups, and glorying in the ride.

She rode every pony on the farm and ventured to break some of the young and untrained colts into docility. This meant climbing onto the saddled back of an unappreciative yearling and hanging on for dear life as the horse thrashed around, trying to unseat the pesky human on its back. It meant hanging on while being tossed, battered and bruised until the pony tired and decided to accept the saddle. It meant walking proudly away from a tamed horse with joy in her heart and an ache in her bones. Often Nan was bucked off a determined colt into a muddy ditch. She would pick herself up, rub the muck off her pants, grab the bridle, and ride the horse again until she won the contest. Then she and the horse would be friends forever.

The year that Nan was thirteen, our mother rented a small house in Athabasca so that Ralph and Margaret could go to high school. Of course, Nan was expected to go along and attend school in town. Instead, she stubbornly insisted on staying at the farm so that she could be with the horses, cows and dogs. She won that argument and remained at home, much to my mother's dismay.

When she was in the twelfth grade, Nan applied at Alberta College. She was accepted, and moved into an apartment in Edmonton with our oldest brother, Dick, who was attending university at the time. In October of that year, disaster struck the family. Our mother contracted pneumonia. The illness took her out of our world with no warning and no time for thought. We were all devastated. Mom had been the sturdy tree trunk from which her children had grown, and though we had spread our branches and become more independent, still we had clung to her solid presence.

After a short hiatus at home, most members of the family had to return to their jobs or school. I was left alone on the farm with Dad and my brother George. I was dangling in space. My father tried to spread a healing salve over my pain, but he found this task very difficult because he had always left the caring of the children to his sweet and gentle wife.

Nan was overcome with worry about me. Against Dad's wishes, she dropped out of school and returned to the farm, promising to finish her school year through a correspondence program. This was an empty promise, as there was too much work to do on the farm for much attention to be given to anyone's studies. I was delighted to have her at home, not realizing the magnitude of the sacrifice she had made for me.

Two years later she enrolled in the School of Nursing at the Royal Alexandra Hospital and was finally started on her career. When I visited her in Edmonton during her years of training, I was bathed in the joyful aura that surrounded her. Her nature was filled with sunshine and she was so pretty, with her wide, radiant smile that took in the whole world.

When she started going out with Leigh, a medical doctor, we all giggled at the prospect of one of our family members landing into affluence. They became engaged and George, ever the wag, announced, "Let's phone Dad and tell him to sell the farm and come on down to the city. Nan's marrying money!" Leigh, who turned out to be a wonderful man and a great husband, could not help but be amused at this bit of wisdom. Nan was busy and happy in her marriage, but she was far from rich in those early years.

I have lived near Nan for almost forty years, and she has always been there to give me help if required, and to laugh with me at the same silly jokes. She still lets emotional reactions take precedence over reason, and she always cares about people. To her, caring is more important than logic.

The High Price of Belonging

When I was in the eleventh grade, I was sent to live with my aunt and uncle in Ponoka, a town that seemed, then, to be quite far from home. My sister Nan wanted to move to Edmonton, and could no longer look after me on the farm. Aunt Nell, much beloved by Dad, was elegant and sweet natured; I do not doubt that Dad hoped her characteristics would rub off on me.

Before my move, I had been attending a school in Athabasca, where I was part of an "in" group. In those expanding years of friendship, my confidence had sprung to life and blossomed.

Then I was flung into a different and intimidating world. My aunt and uncle were kind and good company, so life at home was fine. My schoolwork was interesting and I easily maintained an honours average. Socially, however, things were not so rosy: I hovered on the edge of acceptance. Although my classmates were reasonably friendly, no group of girls invited me into their circle, and no boy showed interest in me. I was let down and assailed by feelings of self-doubt.

There was a particular group of five girls whose friendship I longed for. They were pretty and well dressed, and they always seemed to be having fun. They were pleasant and polite to me, but no matter how hard I tried for inclusion in their company, I remained on the outside.

Finally, in late spring, I had an opportunity to break through this barrier. It was the first warm and bright day of the season, and the sun and wind had banished the snow. The group that I so longed to join was going to play hooky from school; they planned to take their lunches to a secluded spot and then hitch-hike to the neighbouring town of Lacombe. There was no purpose in the trip except the doing of it. Each of these girls had hitchhiked somewhere before, and to them, it was just a lark.

71

Everyone played hooky once in a while, they reasoned, and if they left the school separately no one would notice.

"Are you coming with us?" they asked me impatiently.

I had never before thought of playing hooky; no one at my former school had done it - at least, not to my knowledge. I was beset alternately by doubt and temptation. I really liked school, and I felt I would be disloyal to Aunt Nell if I cut class, for she would be disappointed beyond words if she discovered my inappropriate behaviour. On the other hand, there was the irresistible prospect of finally belonging. I had languished in semi-isolation for most of the year, and here at last was my ticket into that glamorous group. My decision was not long in coming.

We took our lunches and proceeded in pairs to our rendezvous in a small clearing by a little pond. The sun shone down benevolently upon us, and as we munched companionably on our pooled peanut butter, corned beef and egg sandwiches, my pangs of conscience receded. We took off our shoes and squealed as we waded in the icy waters of a small slough, and we talked about boys. Finally we set out on our hitchhiking adventure.

We stood bravely by the side of the highway in three groups of two, thumbs extended, hoping to be picked up by a friendly couple. Janet stood with me - and stood and stood - while the cars whooshed by. At long last, a car stopped behind us and two of the girls climbed into it. Half an hour later, the second pair of girls flashed past us in another car. No one stopped for us. The sun was dropping toward the horizon, and a chill began to fall around us. The prospect of getting a ride to Lacombe seemed less and less appealing.

A carload of yelling, jeering boys finally stopped and shouted at us to pile in. I was very wary of accepting their offer; to my relief, Janet shook her head.

"We're just waiting for our parents," she stammered. I was seized with an overwhelming fear that we might be forced inside this car. The boys, however, roared off with derisive shouts, their car spewing exhaust fumes and flicking up gravel. Our adventure had palled considerably by then.

"Let's go home," I said. "I don't want to go to Lacombe. I think I've missed the school bus to the hospital already!" My aunt and uncle resided on the grounds of the mental hospital, where my uncle worked.

To my relief, Janet meekly agreed, and we plodded back down the highway to town. I had missed the bus, and, tired and cold, we walked the two miles home.

I made up an excuse for my lateness. "I had to get some help with Chemistry," I mumbled to Aunt Nell. My very noticeable sunburn generated further questions, forcing me to manufacture another lie. "We had a track meet today, and I forgot to tell you about it," I offered lamely.

The next day, seated quietly in the first class, I heard my name along with the names of the other culprits in the hooky adventure listed over the loudspeaker system.

"These people are to report immediately to the principal's office," the voice boomed. Retribution was about to fall.

My name was called first, and my heart thudded as I entered the office. Mr. Sutherland, the principal, towered above me and wasted no time in getting to the point. "Where were you yesterday afternoon?" he demanded.

Fed up with my tangled web of deception, I blurted out the truth. "I played hooky," I answered.

"Well, you're suspended from school, as of now. Get your books and leave immediately!" he barked.

Three others must have told the truth as well, because four out of the six of us were ushered ignominiously out the school doors and left shivering on the steps with the words "And don't come back!" echoing in our ears.

We trudged downtown, sobbing and snuffling, and took refuge in a café. We burst forth in loud, unrestrained crying, heedless of other customers. Lots of kids had played hooky before, so why had we been singled out for such harsh punishment? What would our parents - in my case, my aunt and uncle - say? What were we going to do? We sat agonizing over these questions. For me the most terrible thought was of Aunt Nell informing Dad of my delinquency. Would I be sent back to the farm in disgrace, forced to miss the rest of the school year?

I plodded the two miles home, trying to gather my courage. When I arrived, I rushed in, eager to get the dreadful ordeal over with. Amid tears of self-recrimination, I related my sorry tale. Aunt Nell listened calmly. She even told me of a prank or two that she had pulled in her youth.

"However," she said, "the thing that really disappoints me is that you lied to me." Her next words, "and what do you think your father will say when he hears about this?" only reinforced my previous fears.

I talked with some of the girls on the phone and we resolved to try for readmission to school. We learned that two of the girls who had cut class with us had claimed illness and, promising to bring notes from their parents, had escaped all punishment. The next day we made our way to the school, where, after much pleading with the secretaries, we were allowed to see the principal once more.

"We're terribly sorry and ashamed," we chorused. "If you'll only let us back in, we'll work really hard. We'll never play hooky again."

"No!" he snapped. "There's been entirely too much truancy in this school, and it is about to stop. You will serve as an example to any others who may be tempted to follow the same path. You are expelled from school for the remainder of the year. Now collect your books and leave the premises!" His voice grew louder and angrier as he spoke.

Once again, we trudged despondently home. From then on, we lacked the zest even to talk together on the phone. I drooped around my aunt's house, waiting to be summoned back to the farm in abject humiliation. About mid-week, Aunt Nell announced in a matter-of-fact tone that a school board meeting had been called regarding the expelled students and that she was going to attend it.

A small spark of hope kindled within me, though I dared not let it flare too brightly. On the night of the school board meeting, after several of hours of nervous waiting, I heard Aunt Nell's car pull up and her key turn in the lock. I held my breath. In she marched, trying to look severe but unable to suppress a triumphant smile.

"You are going to be readmitted to school and given another chance!" she announced jubilantly.

I flung myself into her arms, amid another flood of tears, this time of gratitude. "How did you get them to listen?" I asked.

"Well, first I explained that your mother had passed away and that your father, my brother, was a widower who lived way up north. He had entrusted you to my care, and I felt very responsible for your welfare. Then I showed the board members your last report card and asked them how anyone could justify depriving such a student of an education because of one lapse in judgment. They voted to reinstate all of the students on the condition that you submit written apologies and promise never to repeat this misdemeanour."

"Oh, thank you!" I cried. "You're wonderful!" The heavy cloud that had been hanging over my shoulders and darkening my world for the past few days suddenly floated off. The only thing that galled me was the fact that two of our "friends" had produced notes from their parents and had escaped punishment.

We returned to school the following Monday, very meek and attentive. Our notoriety faded after a few days, as we had hoped. Intent on proving myself worthy of Aunt Nell's intervention, I worked hard and achieved honours in June. Dad came to attend the awards ceremony. He seemed very proud of me, and never mentioned the hooky escapade. To this day, I don't know if Aunt Nell ever told him about it.

I remained friends with the three girls who had suffered along with me, and in time I found other friends. The aura that had surrounded that elite circle of girls faded and disappeared.

Because of this experience, I have been able to empathize with young people who have felt torn by peer pressure. During my years as a teacher, I tried to be more tolerant than stern when considering the decisions my students had made.

The Prom

My new blue taffeta dress swished against my legs as I dashed to the door and happily threw it open. I was seventeen, just beginning to taste the joys of the adult world, and I was filled with elation at the prospect of going to my high school prom with the most handsome boy in the world.

My smile of greeting faded and my heart seemed to plunge to my toes, for there, on the doorstep, stood Andy Takahara. He wore a navy blue suit with a crisp, white shirt, and a white carnation poked out of his buttonhole. His black hair was slicked back, and he sported a wide, toothy grin. In his hands he clasped a corsage of pale purple orchids. He half bowed as he formally offered it to me.

I stood motionless, rooted to the floor and incapable of greeting him; finally I managed to take the flowers into my trembling hands.

"Come in and sit down," I mumbled, trying to breathe evenly. "I'll be back in a moment."

I fled to the kitchen and hid myself behind its protective walls. Standing at the sink, I bought a little time by pouring myself a glass of cold water. I drank it slowly, staring at the telephone that hung ominously on the wall, waiting for me to end the most wonderful romance of my life.

Andy, the boy I had dumped so unceremoniously in the living room, was a classmate in my twelfth grade class in Edmonton. He was a pleasant boy, and we had become friends that year because we were both strangers in a new school. We had known each other previously, as Andy had sat behind me in our eleventh grade class in Ponoka. We chatted easily when we met in the halls, talking of old friends and teachers, and often we went to the café across the street for a cup of coffee.

I had a real boyfriend named Ron Morrison, who was tall, blond and handsome. I was pleased that from amongst all the girls who had vied for his attention, he had chosen me. He had enlisted in the Air Force in the last year of World War II and had been sent to St. Thomas, Ontario, for his basic training. We wrote letters to each other almost every day, saying how much we missed one another. I had implored him to find a way to come to Edmonton to be my date for my prom and to attend my high school graduation. He replied that he was very sorry, but leave was never granted for such a trivial thing as a graduation. I was depressed, for I felt abandoned by him.

Then one day at school, Andy had approached me timidly, and politely asked if I had a date for the graduation dance.

"Well, no, I don't," I replied offhandedly, wondering why he had asked.

He clasped his hands in front of him and asked with great formality, "Would you consider going with me? I would deem it a great honour."

This was the spring of 1945, and though the war in Europe was over, it still raged on in Japan; a lot of resentment toward Japanese-Canadians seethed under the surface of society. I had noticed many of the other students giving Andy a wide berth. Feeling annoyed at them and also a bit defiant, I smiled at him and replied, "Sure, I'll go with you."

A few days later Ron phoned all the way from St. Thomas with the wonderful news that he was being granted leave; he would be able to come to Edmonton for my graduation, after all. I was delighted, and gloried in the prospect of showing him off to my snooty classmates.

Yet I also worried about how I would tell Andy that my real boyfriend was coming home to be my partner at our prom. I grew more troubled as I tried to find Andy in the school halls. To my dismay, he never appeared. The day of the graduation dance arrived. Feeling desperate, I persuaded one of the school secretaries to give me his phone number and I called his home.

His mother answered in Japanese, though she switched to English as soon as I spoke. "No," she said with a heavy accent, "Andy is not at home. He has an afternoon job."

I blurted out my message quickly, so that my courage would not fade away. "This is Audrey. Would you please tell Andy that I can't go to the graduation dance with him? My real boyfriend will be here, and I'll be going with him."

"Okay," said Andy's mother, not sounding at all dejected. Had she understood my message? I dismissed the thought, not wanting to dwell on such a possibility. Yet there he was, on the night of the dance, waiting in the living room as I stood irresolutely in the kitchen holding his sad little corsage in my hand.

Ron, who would be more charming and handsome than ever in his new blue uniform, would be arriving in less than an hour. I realized that if I moved quickly, I would have just enough time to catch him before he left the hotel to come and pick me up. My romantic dream floated away as I took a deep breath and picked up the phone, dialling the number that Ron had given me.

The hotel receptionist answered. "I'd like to leave a message for Ron Morrison," I said, my voice as strong and clear as I could make it. "This is Audrey. The message is to read 'I am very sorry, but I will not be able to go to the graduation dance with you tonight.'" That was all I could think of to say, so I quickly hung up the receiver.

Taking a deep breath, I pinned on the pale purple orchid, picked up my blue mohair stole and walked into the living room. Suddenly, I felt determined and strangely cheerful. I placed my arm through Andy's as he stood up and smiled.

That night, I discovered that he was a true gentleman with a great sense of humour. The dance, to my surprise, was a remarkably pleasant event. I phoned Ron the next day and left him another message, but he failed to return my call. I never heard a word from him again. Somehow it didn't seem to matter.

79

The Healing Land

Because I grew up on a farm, the feel of the land was in my bones. When I was young, I spent long, sunlit summer days sauntering around the grounds; or I stretched out on a warm patch of grass under our aspen trees, looking through the quivering leaves for patterns in the clouds.

Mom, never far away, was the strength and support of my life. Her love wrapped around me to insulate and protect me from all harm.

Dad was a farmer, and as such his hopes, dreams and spirit blossomed or shrivelled alongside the generosity or stinginess of the land. His bond with the land was strong: he knew every plant, every bird and every creature that crept through the grass and peeked out from the forest floor.

He often took me on walks with him through the meadows, along the roadsides, deep into shady groves, and out across the sweeping expanse of the fields. He was learned in the flora and fauna of our boreal forest, and he loved to share his knowledge with anyone who would listen. I revelled in the attention he gave me, soaking up his teachings like a thirsty sponge. As we walked, he would flip aside green foliage and find the hidden faces of delicate wild flowers. I learned their names as I picked them: crocuses, bluebells, marsh marigolds, Indian paintbrush, and tall, showy fireweed. I proudly carried raggedy bouquets home to my mother, who placed them with great ceremony in a cut-glass vase in the centre of the dining table.

I spent many hours reading on a blanket, beneath the overhanging branches of our Manitoba maples. The vegetable garden was adjacent to this bower of mine, allowing me to munch on newly ripened tomatoes as I read. Sometimes I ventured into the orchard, where Dad experimented in growing fruits that were capable of surviving the rigours of our harsh climate. I picked raspberries, strawberries, Saskatoon berries, red currants, and tart green apples, taking them away to savour under the maples.

At other times, I wandered out into the barnyard to see the farm animals. All of the horses had names and distinct characters. Belle and Dexter were stalwart, sturdy Belgians capable of pulling an enormous load; Jill was a gentle pony who ambled along at a leisurely pace; there was swift Nelly, who had been a race horse before she was winded; and there was Prince, a beautiful half-Belgian sorrel who could clear any fence built by man. There were many other horses, both frisky and staid, and each one was as unique as any of our family members.

The cows were named Daisy, Pet and Roseleaf. I would visit them and stand in the warm air of the barn inhaling the strong odours. Though the stench almost swept me away, the atmosphere provided me with a strange sense of comfort and security.

I passed many hours playing in the yard, the outbuildings and the nearby groves of poplar, spruce and pine. I spied brown rabbits hopping along, unafraid. I saw soft-eyed deer skimming over fences, and big, loose-jawed moose stopping to stare at me before cantering off gracefully through the fields. I saw red foxes flashing into the woods, their bushy tails flaring out behind them. I saw coyotes skulking along the roadsides, and raccoons with their neat black masks. The animals and plants that surrounded me in my childhood were part of my being: they planted the seeds from which my love of the land grew and flourished.

The autumn of my tenth year seemed to be especially beautiful. The trees flaunted their yellow, purple and crimson leaves; dressed in their bright and gaudy finery, the willow, poplar and birch trees were holding a farewell party. The golden wheat, high as my chest, swayed in the fall breeze, and the big threshing machine hungrily chewed up the sheaves that it was fed, only to spew them back in a thick stream of nutty-smelling wheat. Another spout tossed out weightless chaff that fluttered like snow into a tidy round straw stack. The land was benevolent and strewed its generous gifts unto the world.

81

That fall, Mom and I took afternoon lunch into the fields for the threshers. We bounced along in our old car through the barnyard, where horses swished their tails lazily; we passed weathered wooden granaries, and clattered on through rutted fields to the site of the threshing. The men climbed eagerly down from their hayracks and quickly devoured their lunches. They thanked Mom with white smiles from their dusty faces and then headed back to the fields as the dropping sun bathed us in its gentle warmth. The world was a sunlit glade.

Then our mother died, and the world grew dark.

The sun could not force its way through such heavy, tear-filled clouds. The cold and punishing winter set in, matching fate's cruelty. The wind stripped dead leaves from the trees and wailed as it whipped snow around the buildings. Yet the house, the barns and the granaries, accustomed to the force of winter winds, hung on and withstood the rampages of the storms.

The sun came out and sparkled on the dazzling snow, clothing the world in a chilling, fierce beauty. I muddled along, letting melancholy engulf me; sadness clamped my spirit in a hard vice that was as harsh as the winter. Despite suffering in his own grief, Dad tried to cast some light onto my dreary life. He read to me, as Mom had done, and opened the preserves that she had jarred; his efforts only brought tears, however, for I was too immersed in my own misery to respond with warmth.

The winter passed, as all things do, and spring poked its soft nose out into the world. Robins, red-winged blackbirds and meadowlarks appeared, chirping out their melodic songs. Way up in the clear northern air, skeins of Canada geese sailed through the sky, calling "ah-honk, ah-honk" to their travelling companions. Thick grasses and reeds shot up along the ditches and at the edges of small ponds. Aspens and willows donned soft, lime-green leaves, while spruce, and pines sent out velvety sprigs that signalled a renewal of life.

Often, I sat by myself, letting loneliness and sorrow swallow me. Then one day, as I sat on a log beside a small stream, the beauty of the land sifted through my crusty shell and awakened my senses. Nature's nimble fingers shredded the shawl of my grief, and a gauzy lightness descended upon my shoulders. I experienced a sort of epiphany, brought about by the land.

I dipped my fingers into the bubbling water among mosses, water lilies, frogs' eggs that felt like gobs of tapioca pudding, and tiny tadpoles that shot around like bullets. Frogs hopped from one leaf to another, croaking at me for disturbing their busy world. A little brown rabbit sat as still as a stone, then bounced away. Above me a red-headed woodpecker sounded out "bonk, bonk, clack, clack," as he chipped out a hole in a tree. Small brown sparrows shot off as raucous blue jays swooped down and soared back up into the trees. Bog violets, white daisies and glistening yellow dandelions brightened the earth around me.

The beauty of the land, with its power of renewal, seeped into my heart, washing away my distress. I felt my mother's spirit flow into mine, and I sensed her saying, "The world is good. Love it. Live it, for me. I am near you." I knew then I would survive.

I was entranced by the world around me once again. I saw the wildflowers spring up; I saw the fledgling birds taking their first flights; I felt the downy wings of baby chicks as their wee feet prickled my hand. I went for nature walks with Dad. While I shared in his sorrow, I felt his joy in the perfection of the land, as well. I understood that Mom's spirit would always be with me, and that the land would nourish my soul.

The years slipped away and I grew into maturity. I went home to visit Dad on weekends and summer vacations; he always seemed to be overjoyed to see me. Then, in my last year at university, he had a heart attack. As suddenly as Mom had left, he was gone from the earth. My brothers and sisters and I buried him beside our mother. The land that he had loved claimed him and took his body back into its arms. I missed my conversations with him, his knowledgeable lectures on seemingly any subject, and I missed his wry, self-deprecating humour. He had taught me many things, and his spirit lives on to give me guidance.

Peace River Adventure

My friend Margie Gans and I were to teach in rural schools in the Peace River region during the months of May and June. We had completed but one year of university; however, due to a teacher shortage in the province of Alberta, we were issued "letters of authority" permitting us to teach. We felt both apprehension and excitement as we headed off to begin our careers. It would be an adventure - and it would provide us with nice little nest eggs for the coming year.

Mr. Dean, the charming school superintendent who had interviewed us in Edmonton, had assured us that pleasant living accommodations could be arranged. Margie was to have a teacherage, a little house of her own, and I was to board at a farmhouse near my school. Teachers had boarded sometimes at my home when I was a child, and I envisioned a similar situation: a sprawling, comfortable place with a welcoming atmosphere.

Although we felt nervous about the jobs we were beginning - and especially about facing such a sea of children, ranging from first to eighth graders - we wasted no time worrying about our living accommodations. We revelled in the challenge as we waved goodbye to our friends and boarded the Northern Alberta Railway train. It was evening when we clattered away from Edmonton, and we spent an interminable night in a noisy, grimy passenger car that clanged and lurched through the darkness. We arrived in our destination of Fairview feeling tired and unkempt, though eager to spread our wings in our chosen careers. Mr. Dean, acting somewhat less effusive than when he had first hired us, met us at the station and piled our luggage into his car. Off we went!

Margie's teacherage was the first stop on our route. When we arrived, we could only stare incredulously at the scene before us. That couldn't be what she was expected to live in, I thought. It was a lonely, one-room log shack surrounded by bush on every side. Inside, it was even less appealing: its furniture consisted of a homemade wooden bed with a bare straw tick for a mattress, a battered wooden table with two chairs and a rusty woodstove - that was it! The walls and floor were of unpainted boards; one sooty window filtered in the only light. The sole ornamentation in the place was an outdated calendar with curled corners featuring an impossibly beautiful blonde in a red satin dress. It was not a sight to gladden the heart of a university student. Poor Margie looked about to cry.

While I felt sorry for my friend, I thanked the Good Lord that I wouldn't have to live in such a dreadful place myself. Leaving her standing alone and forlorn on the stoop, I jumped back into the car and Mr. Dean and I headed for my promised haven in the wilderness.

We bounced along bumpy dirt roads and up to the rutted yard of the farmhouse that was to be my home for two months. A dilapidated shack with a stovepipe sticking up drunkenly from its roof met my horrified eyes. Pieces of broken machinery littered the yard, and pigs, chickens and ducks wandered freely up to the doorstep. A stout, weather-beaten woman in a dirty cotton dress and rubber boots emerged from within.

Her words of welcome did little to hearten me. "Well, it's time ya got here!" she grumbled. "I shoulda gone fer the cows by now, but I hadda wait fer you. Didn't want no teacher anyways, but there ain't no other place fer you to stay, so here ya are. An' I'll tell ya right now there ain't nothin' fancy about our place, so if you're too fussy, you better turn around right now and be on yer way. It's thirty dollars a month if ya stay."

With that, she turned and stomped back into the house. I followed her reluctantly, picking my way through the debris in the yard while Mr. Dean quietly eased himself into the background. The inside of the house was even more appalling than the outside. The fetid and gagging stench of the chickens was overwhelming; they clucked their way around the kitchen freely, perching on the stairs or the table, bickering over scraps on the floor. Overcome with nausea, I turned to flee the house.

The landlady stood in the doorway, hands on hips and elbows protruding belligerently. "Not good enough fer you, eh? I figgered that when I seen you!" Grudgingly, she let me pass, and I started out toward the spot where the car had been parked, intent on venting my indignation at the deceitful superintendent who had brought me to this place. Instead, I could only stare in disbelief at my two suitcases deposited in the dirt and the cloud of dust stirred up by Mr. Dean's rapid retreat. I had no choice but to bring my suitcases into the house and try to mollify the hostile landlady.

I managed to endure one night in that house. The next day, I posted a note on the school door announcing that classes would start the following morning; then I walked ten miles to the town of Whitelaw. At the hardware store, I was fortunate enough to find a secondhand bicycle. I bought it for twenty dollars and rode off to Margie's little log teacherage.

"I'm going to stay with you and ride the thirteen miles to my school every day," I blubbered after trying to describe my "boarding place" to her. I looked around the teacherage that I had so disdained the day before. Margie had cleaned it up and had added a few personal touches, including a bedspread, a tablecloth, a curtain, and several pictures on the walls. It looked quite inviting! She had met some neighbours who were kind enough to fetch my suitcases from my offensive landlady's house.

The rest of our two-month stay turned out to be a pleasant experience. I left the teacherage at seven o'clock each morning and rode to school in the perfect brightness of a spring morning in the country. As the season progressed, the poplar and birch trees turned a beautiful pale green, the frogs croaked in the ditches, and the robins and sparrows sang to me along the way. At the end of the school day, I cycled home through the soft air. After supper we would go for walks, visit the friendly couple up the road, or simply sit and talk or read. It rained twice while we were there, making the roads too slick for my bicycle, and on those days a kindly neighbour drove me to and from school.

My worries about teaching turned out to be unfounded. The students had been without a teacher for a whole year, and they were so glad to have me that the little ones clung to me, while the older ones kept trying to outdo each other at being helpful. They were eager to learn and, fortunately, were unaware of how ill-prepared I was for my task, with only two years of teacher training under my belt. The two months sped by, and I was sorry when it was time to leave.

On the way home I stopped in at the School Division office to see Mr. Dean. When I protested his earlier treatment of me, he rather shamefacedly admitted that he had sped away from my horrible boarding house that day with only self-preservation in mind. So much for the honour Of government officials!

Washroom Caper

I stood nervously beside the big mahogany door of the men's washroom in the Education Building at the University of Alberta, hoping that it was finally empty. In one of my more absent-minded moments, I had deposited my winter boots in the men's washroom rather than in the ladies', and now I had to retrieve them. The building had been designed so that the men's and women's washrooms switched places between the second and third floors. Really, who paid attention to the floor one was on?

As the building lacked lockers, many girls frequently left their boots in the women's washroom during classes. In the freezing Edmonton winters, we wore heavy, fleece-lined boots that kept our feet from freezing on the long walks to the Education Building; they became hot and itchy when worn indoors. Throughout the winter, the floor of the ladies' washroom was littered with a helter-skelter heap of women's boots.

Being very late for class on that particular day, I dashed into the washroom, used the facilities without a sidewise glance, dropped my boots, and ran out the door to class. As I emerged I noticed two men eying me curiously. I looked down at my clothes to see if anything was amiss. Finding nothing wrong, I shrugged off their looks and slipped into Psychology class. Dr. Dunlop was stomping back and forth across the front of the room in his usual fashion, lecturing about perception and learning and periodically spitting out the word "Gestalt" in small explosions (he seemed to love that word; it was thorny, like his disposition).

His voice, though assailing my ears, failed to engage my mind that day. I began to think of my boots on the washroom floor. Curiously, I did not recall seeing any other pairs of boots around mine. The realization of my mistake suddenly flooded my mind, making me blush violently. Oh, for heaven's sake, I'd really goofed! I was on the *second* floor: I had put my boots in the men's room, not the ladies'! It was no wonder those fellows had looked at me so strangely. I spent the rest of the period trying to devise a plan for extricating my boots from the inappropriate place in which I had deposited them.

As my next class was in another building, five blocks away, I had to walk in flimsy high-heeled pumps through the snow and ice. At the end of the day, I teetered back to the Education Building, my feet numb. I stationed myself warily near the door of the men's room and waited for the coast to clear.

At long last, having seen no one enter or exit the room for some time, I opened the door a crack and peeked inside. There didn't appear to be anyone inside, so I gingerly edged myself in. I peered around the alcove wall and saw my boots, alone and innocently out of place beside the urinals. I was in the act of reaching for them when a nice-looking young man emerged from a cubicle, nonchalantly doing up his fly. I crouched, glued to the floor in my stooped position, unable to move either backward or forward. The man's eyes widened when they lit on me; then he adjusted his pants, made a welcoming gesture and grinned.

"Men's washroom," he announced. "May I help you?"

Feeling my face grow red, I pointed to the boots and stammered, "These are mine!" I snatched them up clumsily.

"Help yourself," he said, still smiling. His smile broadened as he politely ushered me into the hall. As I observed his body beginning to shake with laughter, my nervous tension drained away. First we giggled and then we howled, leaning against the walls to keep erect through our spasms of laughter. Finally, he shook his head and walked off down the hall. I was relieved when I did not run into him again for a long time - the washroom encounter was an embarrassing event that I would sooner like to forget.

Mystery Man

In my final year at university I was registered in Educational Psychology, taught by Dr. Dunlop. Unfortunately, Dr. Dunlop was a man who lacked the skill to clarify anything. In his lectures, he tended to embellish each fact to such an extent that a simple idea would become a dreadful jumble of information. The unit on statistics was a particularly difficult one for me to grasp: I simply could not navigate the zigzag paths he forged in class.

One afternoon after classes, I was walking down a hallway when I heard a male voice in one of the classrooms talking about statistics. Listening to him outside the door, I discovered that this man was going over the unit in Psychology class that was causing me so much worry. I slipped into the room and asked him if I could join the study group.

"Sure," the young man replied, and went on with his explanation. As he was writing on the blackboard, the half-dozen men who were listening scribbled hastily on their clipboards. Our instructor looked familiar to me, but I could not place him. Since there were more than two hundred students in Dr. Dunlop's class, I assumed that I had seen him there. I was just glad that I had found someone who could make statistics understandable.

I visited this room every afternoon for three weeks, until the fog that had once obscured statistics blew off, allowing the figures to emerge clear and bright. I didn't know the name of the student who tutored me each day, though I was extremely grateful for his help. When Dr. Dunlop finished the unit, we were tested in an exam; it was so simple, and I was sure that I had not made any mistakes when writing it.

After Dr. Dunlop had marked the papers, we retrieved them one by one from a pile on his desk. When it was my turn to pick up my paper, he asked, "Couldn't you do any better than that?" I was embarrassed and looked inside the booklet to see my mark. It was a perfect score! I blushed as Dr. Dunlop announced that mine was the only paper to earn a mark of one hundred percent. I wondered why the young man who had explained statistics for me had not written a perfect paper, as well. I looked for him amongst the departing students.

He came up to me and smiled. "I'm glad you aced this exam," he said. "I made a stupid error and got ninety-eight percent." He shrugged.

His smile was oddly familiar, and I had the sudden suspicion that he was the man I had met in the men's washroom when I was retrieving my boots. I didn't say as much to him, however, remembering how mortified I had felt that day. I didn't encounter him again that year, and I gradually pushed him out of my thoughts.

A New Start

My first year of teaching was an unmitigated disaster. A recent university graduate, I was filled with high hopes and enthusiasm for my new career, and thought that high school English and French would be a good place to begin. A newspaper want ad listed these courses, and I sent off my application to the chairman of the school board in Mirror, a town unknown to me. It was not long before I received a reply of acceptance. How I later wished that I had never seen that ad.

The students, knowing that I was young and inexperienced, were ready to test me. They were practiced in the art of teacher torment and I was fair game. I fought each day to maintain some level of discipline, but I seldom won the battle. I could never predict what manner of object would fly through space toward me next - chalk, apples, paper airplanes, or donuts. Eventually, I learned to reach up and snatch them as they sailed over my head. My skill in snagging these missiles sometimes impressed the kids, though little else in my bag of tricks did.

I remember lecturing on the topic of the barbarians' arrival in Europe amid a flurry of flying objects. I interposed the suggestion that the barbarians had also sent their progeny to Alberta. Some of the students giggled in response; most were undeterred in their aim to defeat me and send me packing. Somehow, I persevered until June, when I submitted my resignation with heartfelt thanks to God for getting me through that terrible year.

Later that summer I accepted a position in the town of Edson. I decided to give the teaching business another try, and if the second year was no better, I would firmly close the door on it forever. A few days before the start of classes, I was to attend a staff meeting at the school. The school was new and parts of it were still under construction; indeed, all of the classrooms were out of bounds. I looked around for the office, but saw only piles of lumber, sawhorses and pink insulation. There must be a make-shift office somewhere, I thought, and started to explore.

At the end of a hall I heard voices. Following them, I arrived at a room that had the word "GIRLS" printed boldly on its door. Since I felt I into fit this category, I stepped carefully inside. There I saw Mr. Meade, the principal, seated on a white porcelain toilet with a small worktable placed primly before him. Upon my entrance, he stood up, moving aside the table, and graciously extended his hand.

"Welcome to our school, Audrey," he said, smiling kindly. "Meet your fellow teachers: this is Percy Wells, and this is Frances Ciciarelli. They teach junior high. Jack Reid teaches high school Math and Science," Mr. Meade continued, "but he's playing baseball right now, so he'll be along to meet you later." The two teachers to whom I had been introduced sat calmly on the toilets next to Mr. Meade. Percy Wells rose to greet me, and Miss Ciciarelli graciously extended her hand. Both of them were acting as though a bathroom was a normal place to hold a staff meeting.

"Sorry about the surroundings," Mr. Meade said. "The classrooms will be finished when school opens, and the office will be ready soon after. In the meantime, have a seat." He pointed to the third toilet in the row. Hesitating, I then sat down very cautiously. Another teacher, Mrs. Jackson, entered and was introduced to me as she calmly ensconced herself on the fourth toilet. There still remained one vacant toilet; I presumed it was for the privileged Mr. Reid, who was allowed to play baseball instead of attending a staff meeting. As I perched on my toilet, I hoped that everything at my new school would turn out to be this informal.

Then, Jack Reid breezed in, dressed in a dusty baseball uniform. He smiled as he dropped onto the last toilet. He was introduced to me by Mr. Meade. I recognized him immediately.

"I remember you," Jack said, holding out his hand. "You're the girl who got a perfect score in statistics after *I* explained it to you." He grinned, obviously holding no grudge.

I was very strict and aloof in my early days of teaching in that town, for I was constantly fearful of disruptions. The students, however, were very eager to learn: they answered the questions that I posed and they even did their homework. No objects soared over my head, and no dead mice squished under me as I sat down at my desk. My tension gradually eased and I actually began to enjoy teaching again.

Jack, the other high school teacher, was easygoing and friendly. As I was never sure that he was the man of the university washroom incident, I did not mention it to him. An hour or so after the end of every school day, he would come sweeping into my room as I sat preparing the next day's lesson. "You can't work all the time! Let's go for coffee," he would say, whisking me away from my chores.

As the year progressed, any worries I might have had about my teaching abilities dissolved. In May, carefree Jack asked me to marry him; I didn't hesitate in my response. My second year as a teacher was a very good year indeed.

A Shadow Descended

I was married, had a family and was living a busy life in a man-made city. Sometimes, I was so distracted by it all that I forgot about the land outside the city limits. I tried to take our two little girls to the farm often, for as long as it remained in the family. They held out sugar lumps for the horses and scattered grain for the chickens. They watched little calves frisk after their mothers. We wandered through the meadows, and I tried to remember the names of the wildflowers as we picked them.

Whenever I was angry or stressed during these years in the city, I would find the time to return to nature. I would follow a narrow, leaf-lined path that led from our neighbourhood to a little creek that bubbled along, reflecting the sun. Peace would spread over me and I could return, renewed, to my busy world.

Then ill fate struck us a cruel blow. Our beautiful little four-year-old child died, suddenly and unexpectedly, of complications that arose during a routine tonsillectomy. She died in the depths of winter, when the land was cold and hostile. My lovely world was shattered, smashed into a million shards; pain and grief consumed me. I trapped myself in a shell that was as brittle as the winter, and I dwelled in this place without thoughts or feelings or air to breathe.

There was no outside help in those days, no one to relieve my pain. Grief counsellors had not yet appeared on the scene to encourage people to talk out their sorrow. There was no group of parents who had suffered similar losses to offer the comfort of shared pain. Almost no one spoke of our child's death; it was as though she had never existed. A few people were perceptive enough, or strong enough, to mention her name and express their sorrow. Although their words were a lifeline thrown to me when I was drowning, I could only cry in response. Many well-meaning people were afraid to open such a dreadful wound, so they shied away from discussing it and left us alone with our beaten spirits.

I immersed myself in happier lives through books, surfacing only briefly to tend to the needs of our other little daughter. She brought friends home from school each afternoon, trying to dispel the gloom that enshrouded our home. While she succeeded in creating small windows of sunlight into my world, any happiness vanished the moment she was out of sight. I fear I was only half a mother to her in that dark time. I spread layer after layer of plaster over my grief until it was hidden behind a thick wall. When I was alone, my inner ache would chip away the coats of plaster and break out. I let it tumble onto my shoulders until I was pinned down, unable to move.

Jack was fortunate enough to have a job that focused his thoughts for part of the day, but I was left alone in the same house where once my smallest child's piping voice had dwelled, filling me with joy. All I had now was grief. Women who are drowned in sorrow tend to be avoided by society, for they cast a shadow that dims the vibrant world. I stayed inside the house and withdrew more and more into myself, gaining no comfort from people or the land.

In the fullness of time came spring, and I found some ease in tramping down to the little creek that gurgled along to join the river. I sat on a stone by the water and let the soothing elixir of the land treat my illness. Slowly, I was able to take hold of the world again. Tears for my loss have always stayed close to the surface, however. Forty years later, they still lurk in my heart.

While we still live in the city today, I have managed to stay close to the land. Jack and I built a cottage that is nestled among poplar and spruce trees on the shores of crystalline Sylvan Lake. When calm, the waters of the lake are glassy, reflecting the puffy white clouds of the sky and the dark green fringe of trees on the opposite bank. As day draws to a close, they mirror the rose, orange and lavender hues of the sunset. I can relax and absorb the peace of these placid moods.

When a wind blows up, the lake becomes riled; it takes on a threatening grey shade and churns itself into a froth to let the world know of its strength. Then I am cautious and stay on the shore, for in the past nature's power has stamped its mark indelibly upon me.

We spend the weekends and summers at this lake, close to nature, living between the green shore and the azure dome of the sky. My love for the land is constantly being fertilized and watered, and it is always blossoming anew. Nature helps me accept what has been and what will be. It has nurtured and comforted me, and it is the fountainhead of my strength.

Putting on the Dog

Silver and crystal glittered in the light of the sparkling chandelier. I had burnished every item of silverware I possessed; I had taken down every teardrop of cut glass that dangled from the chandelier, scoured it, polished it, and reattached it, pleased with the glow that diffused over the dining-room table. Our best china was arrayed on a white linen cloth that I had starched and ironed with great care. A fragrant arrangement of red roses and pink and blue carnations was nestled among white daisies and soft greenery in the centre of the table. The blue candles in their silver candelabra matched the blue dye that I had sprayed on the white carnations. Every wine glass we owned - and a few I had borrowed - sat on the server waiting to be filled with the red and white nectars of the gods.

I was fairly new on staff at Alberta College. As I wanted to make a favourable impression on the seasoned teachers and administrators, I decided to have a dinner party. Our house was also new, and I wanted to show it in its best light. As the day of the party dawned, I felt a little nervous: we rarely entertained groups of thirty or forty people and I habitually forgot essential items for even the smallest of dinners. This time, I had prepared all the dishes beforehand and had them warm and waiting for their final touches. As I looked over the table, I felt more at ease. We had thought of everything. The dinner would go off without a hitch and I would be proved capable. My reputation for absent-mindedness had been steadily growing at school; finally, it would be erased!

"Now I'll have a leisurely bath and relax," I thought. I had about two hours before the guests would arrive - enough time to dispel the tension that had begun to gnaw at me. I turned on the water in the master bath and then dashed downstairs to make sure that all the rooms were tidy. In a messy pile on the laundry room floor I found the newspapers that had been wrapped

98

around the flowers. I slipped out into the garage to stow them in the garbage. I had gone through the connecting door countless times that busy day, keeping it unlocked for convenience.

This time, as I stepped into the garage and let the door go, I heard the ominous click of the lock behind me. I grasped at the doorknob in panic, but my tugging was in vain. The door remained locked defiantly in my face. Jack had gone to the mall and had locked it securely in his usual careful way. I ground my teeth at his cautious nature.

I could hear the water thundering through the pipes as I stood in the unheated garage, shivering in my flimsy t-shirt. I took heart when I remembered that we had hidden a key outside in the chimney, where the ashes were gathered from the fireplace. The day was frigid, so I scooted around the house, opened the little metal door, and groped for the key in its magnetized box. I should have found it adhered to the inside of the door. My fingers met only cold steel. My heart began to thump with panic as I dug among the ashes. Visions of bath water surging over the tub's edge and flooding the floor flashed through my mind. I ran to the neighbours' house and frantically explained my plight. They smiled and lent me a coat, but could only suggest that I break a window and climb in.

The time was passing and I was growing desperate. I pushed a sawhorse into the deep snow under the laundry room window, took a broom - the only weapon I could find - and smacked at the frosty pane. The glass glittered coldly at me, refusing to yield. I found a hoe and whacked at it again. No luck. I scratched through the snow and found a few pebbles that I fired with all my strength. They clattered against the house and skittered away with no effect. The window was as solid as tempered steel.

When I saw our car approaching at last, I ran into the street waving my arms at Jack like a maniac. I couldn't get the words out fast enough to spur him into action.

"The door's locked and the tub's running!" I shouted. He finally understood, sprinted to the door with key in hand and threw it open. We ran upstairs, only to be met by a torrent of water pouring out of the tub and spreading over the bedroom floor. I turned off the tap and we began to scoop at the pools of water on the rug with dustpans. We threw all the towels we could find over the floor and dashed downstairs. What had happened below the deluge? We were almost afraid to look - the dining room was directly below the tub.

A quarter of the ceiling hung like a huge mixing bowl. Water streamed out of it and on to the table, the server and the floor. The white tablecloth was soaked through, the dishes held puddles of water and the wine glasses were neatly filled with yellowish bath water. Jack placed a pail on the floor, then mounted a chair and poked a hole in the bottom of the ceiling bowl in order to let the water drain out faster. New torrents of water gushed down and filled the container.

What would we do about our party, about the floor, about the bulging, wet ceiling hanging dangerously close to our heads? We weren't sure, but we knew we'd better do something. Our guests would be arriving in about an hour. I threw the dishes and the wine glasses into the dishwasher and then tossed the dripping tablecloth into the dryer. We started sopping up the water from the table, the server and, finally, the squishy rug under our feet. I used a hair dryer in an attempt to dry the ceiling but soon abandoned that, as the gooey white plaster continued to sag and drip on our heads.

I rushed upstairs to get out of my damp and grungy t-shirt and into a dress. No bath this time. It was now getting close to the time for the guests to arrive. I dashed downstairs, whipped the tablecloth out of the dryer and spread it on the table, having no time to iron it. We unloaded the dishwasher and slapped the dishes and wine glasses onto the table and server. The doorbell clanged. Thirty or so of our guests arrived in rapid succession.

100

Trying to look calm, we ushered them into the living room and family room.

"Don't bother taking off your shoes. We're sure they're clean," we chimed, hoping to avoid having people step onto our soggy carpet in their stocking feet. Jack served drinks from a small table that we had brilliantly set up in the living room earlier in the afternoon.

Finally everyone was there, milling about and chatting amiably. The food that I laid out on the dining table looked delicious. I turned down the dimmer switch on the lamp to its lowest level and lit the candles with the hope that no one would notice the sagging ceiling or the damp stain on the rug.

Our guests lined up and made their way around the table. Just as I thought we might get through the catastrophe unscathed, a big blob of water landed on the forehead of one of the guests. She peered up and exclaimed, "Look, the ceiling's falling!"

Jack and I had to tell the sorry tale of our misadventure. Everyone hooted with laughter as they tiptoed around beneath the leaking bowl in the ceiling. The story of my party was told and retold at the school. That was when I gave up putting on the dog -he was destined to piddle on my rug.

Always Young

My father-in-law was named Wilbert, but his friends called him Bert. He was built like a small tank: he stood five-foot-two, weighed two hundred and thirty pounds and was nearly all muscle. His massive shoulders brushed the doorjambs as he moved through a doorway; when he stood, his sturdy legs were planted wide apart to balance his bulky body. His body was a solid block, with his white head like a knob anchored firmly upon his thick neck. His hands were as strong as vices, and his hearty handshake sent a shot of pain through the hand of any unprepared greeter. Throughout his life, he had never backed off from a fight - though there had been few to challenge him. Rarely had his sons considered defying his rules or disputing his opinions.

He was a tough old codger who tolerated little nonsense and abhorred waste. After the death of his wife in the depths of the Depression, he had been left alone to raise two small sons. He had made it through with much work, worry, sweat, and scrimping. Those lean years had scarred his soul, and he could not leave that era behind even during the better times that followed. In his later years, visiting the homes of his sons, he found our contemporary lifestyles too extravagant. The credit cards that we used so casually were an abomination in his eyes; according to him, they would surely bring ruin upon our heads. He never stayed long with us as our wasteful ways bothered him. He was much more comfortable in his small house.

Bert had another side, however, for in his heart he was an adventurer. He had lived life on the edge when he was young, and he would suddenly drop his taciturn expression for a wide grin when drawn into recounting some of those early adventures.

During one of his visits, our son and a friend were outside playing ball, creating such a racket that we could hardly talk. After the commotion had subsided, Bert began to chuckle.

"Those kids can sure make a lot of noise," he commented. "But they can't yell half as loud as I could when I was a shill."

"You were a shill?" I asked, amazed. I couldn't imagine Bert in such a role.

"Sure I was! And I'll tell you how it came about. My dad got real mad at me once for tearing up my pants. It wasn't my fault, and I got mad right back at him. That didn't get me anywhere, so I ran away and joined the circus."

"The *circus*," I repeated, amazed. Jack had never told me this fact about his father. "How old were you?" I asked.

"Fourteen, going on fifteen," he announced, rather proudly.

"You were just a kid. What did you do in the circus?" I asked.

"Well, I would stand outside a tent and yell about all the exciting things to see, like bearded ladies and two-headed calves. 'Course it was all lies, but it brought the people in. Nobody expects the truth at a circus, anyway.

"Later, I learned to ride a trick motorcycle in a velodrome; I did that for a few months until I smashed myself up and had to go home to recover. I hung around home for a while working for my dad and playing baseball. I was a pretty good ballplayer in those days," he said with a smile. "I got scouted by a guy from the Chicago Cubs' farm team. I played for them for a whole summer. I think I could have made the major leagues," he said wistfully, "but I got hit in the knee by a baseball and had to give up the game."

"Then did you go home again?" I asked. I didn't want him to dwell on this misfortune.

"Yeah," he said. "The War was on. I joined up."

"How old were you then?" It seemed to me he must have been too young to be recruited.

"Only seventeen. No one seemed to care about your age in those days. You just had to write 'eighteen' in the blank space and you were in. Some guys got into the army at fifteen."

"Were you in all that trench warfare?" I had never been told what he did in the War, and wondered how he had gone through that dreadful time.

"Yep. I was at Passchendaele, Vimy Ridge and the Somme," he said slowly, as his face lost its glow.

"What did you do there? Were you in the infantry?" I had never imagined him in the sodden trenches among the rats.

"I was a runner. Being short and close to the ground, I could sprint real fast from one camp to another to deliver messages."

"Were you shot at?" I asked. I was thinking of war movies I had seen with artillery barrages mowing down young soldiers like stalks of wheat. In one, the soldiers peered over the edge of the trenches, let off some shots and ducked down to dodge returning fire; then they fell and lay dead in the soaking fields.

"Oh, yeah, I was shot at all the time. I learned to dart between trees and crawl on my belly along the ground. I was lucky because I never got hit, but lots of my pals were shot or blown up. They died out there in the muddy fields. My brother was killed three months before Armistice Day." His eyes watered as he sat still and quiet, staring off into the distance. I realized why he didn't speak much about those years.

"What did you do when you weren't carrying messages?" I asked, hoping to draw him out of his sadness and bring him back to happier times.

"Oh, we used to play rummy or poker in the trenches. I could usually clean out all the other guys," he chuckled. Once again, he fell silent with his reminiscences, though this time with a smile. Could the adventuresome young soldier really be the same stern taskmaster of my husband's youth, or the grumpy old man whom we called Grampa? It seemed beyond belief.

Our son suddenly burst into the house with his ball and glove. Bert's eyes lit up. He hoisted himself out of his chair and headed outside with all the speed he could muster.

"Come on, son: let's play ball!" he shouted, and I believed.

Our Last Camping Trip

The rain pelted down and water splattered from our car's wheels as they swished through murky puddles. If the weather was a bad omen, we took no notice of it. Jack, our two children and I waved confidently to our neighbours, who were peering at us through their steamy windows as we drove down our street. Our wonderful new tent trailer glided obediently behind the car. We were taking a trip, travelling from our home in Edmonton to Toronto, down to New York, up to Montréal, and then back to Alberta via the Prairies.

I revelled in the prospect of seeing most of Canada, as well as the bright lights of Broadway. Carol, then seventeen years old, was cajoled into enthusiasm for the trip by the prospect of shopping at Saks Fifth Avenue (though what she hoped to buy in such a store, I couldn't say). Seven-year-old Rob was easy to please: he had never been camping and this was an adventure! Jack, on the other hand, had taken many trips to eastern Canada and New York through his job. He wanted to give the rest of us the chance to see these cities and the beautiful landscapes between them for ourselves.

By the end of the first day, our spirits, like our bodies, were dampened. The deluge continued unabated until we reached Lloydminster, a town that straddles the Alberta-Saskatchewan border. As camping was impossible, we decided to stay in a motel. However, the downpour had wreaked havoc on the town: it was awash in water, and the streets had become rushing creeks. Roads were barricaded so that no vehicle could cross into the east side of town. After splashing up and down every street on the west side of these roadblocks, we found only one motel. It was dilapidated and uninviting, but we had no choice. We sloshed into the lobby and registered.

Our tiny suite was both drab and damp. As we stepped into it, we discovered that the rain had seeped in through the windows and doorway, leaving a soggy rug that squished under our feet. From the "kitchenette" there emanated the cloying odour of stale grease and rotten potatoes. Searching for the source of this foul scent, we looked under the sink and discovered a bag of grey and mouldy potatoes sprouting long white tentacles. We tossed them outside and I sprayed clouds of Chanel No. 5 into the air to cover the stench.

After having eased our hunger pangs with cheese and crackers, we crawled warily into bed, trying our best to avoid touching any of the room's more dirt-encrusted surfaces.

"Mom, my sheets are full of holes," Rob exclaimed as he pulled back his covers. Sure enough, they looked as though moths or mice had been chewing at them.

"Shut your eyes and go to sleep," his dad replied without compassion.

"It stinks in here!" Rob said, trying again for sympathy

"Here," I answered, spraying his sheets with more perfume.

He gave up and dropped off to sleep. Somehow, we all managed to do the same.

We awoke to a bright morning and dashed thankfully to our car. Our spirits lifted as we splashed through the receding puddles into a glittering, sun-filled world. We were soon making our way across the wide Prairies. It was not long before the children tired of gazing at the endless expanse of flat land. Carol buried herself in a novel while Rob drew in his colouring book and played with his cars on a track his dad had built for him.

The road was a lonely grey ribbon of asphalt, stretched across the sun-browned face of the Saskatchewan plain. Mile after mile of waving grain extended ahead of us. The wide sweep of the horizon was broken here and there by little towns with towering elevators, modern farms with big barns and silos, or tumbledown farmhouses. Eddies of dust spun around these neglected memen-

106

tos. We wondered about the fate of the settlers, who had built these homes with such high hopes. In all likelihood, the Great Depression had wreaked its destruction upon these families, too.

It was our first evening of using the trailer. I opened one of the cupboards only to have a shower of china shards come crashing down upon me - no one had warned us that we should pack only *plastic* dishes for our trip! We swept up the mess and headed for a hardware store, where we found a compact set of camping dishes.

We continued eastward, setting up our trailer each night. We slept soundly, refreshed by the soft, grain-scented air that sifted through the canvas walls.

When we got to Winnipeg, however, our sleeping conditions changed for the worse. Recent high waters had generated clouds of mosquitoes that clogged our ears and noses as we tried to sleep. The next morning, eager to escape these voracious little beasts, we set off in great haste.

We passed through North Dakota and Minnesota, and continued southward around Lake Michigan. We sat silent and white-knuckled as Jack slowly navigated the cumbersome trailer through Chicago, where cars blasted their horns and zipped impatiently around us.

We headed north to Canada through Detroit. We stopped in the city to do laundry; having no knowledge of the reputations of certain districts, we blundered into a very bad area. A gang of scruffy, belligerent-looking youths seemed to have commandeered the laundromat, and they swaggered around waving switchblades in the air. When they flashed their weapons menacingly in our direction, we panicked and pulled our dripping clothes from the washer. Leaving pools of soapy water spreading across the floor, we tossed the clothes in a plastic bag and threw it into the trunk of the car, then sped away. We resolved to survey the next laundromat before venturing into it.

We passed through Windsor and finally reached Toronto, the jewel in Canada's crown - at least according to Torontonians. We found it clean and fresh, its busy streets bustling with activity and comfortably unthreatening. We shopped in the boutiques of Yorkville and strolled along the waterfront.

We headed east through Buffalo toward New York City. Deciding it would not be wise to venture into New York with a trailer, we left it at a campground. Thank goodness we did. After navigating our perilous way through the city to our hotel we abandoned the car until it was time to leave - the traffic was terrifying, even in a taxi.

We did the usual tourist things in New York: peered at the Statue of Liberty, surveyed the city from the top of the Empire State Building, saw *Mame* on Broadway, and shopped at Bloomingdale's, Macy's and Saks. Carol spent all the money she had been allotted for the trip on one shirt from Saks.

Tired and anxious to see Canada again, we resumed our journey to Montréal. Carol frequently brought out the trendy creation she had bought in New York and fingered it lovingly, while warning her little brother that she would break his arm if he so much as touched it with his grubby little fingers.

That evening when we got back to our trailer, the children and I were laid low by a type of flu or food poisoning. It was Jack's birthday, and the poor man sat alone with a powdery cake from a convenience store while the children and I rushed back and forth to the outhouse. It was raining, and I had to make so many trips to the toilet that I was drenched, and gave up changing my clothes. On one such trip, my need was so urgent that I attempted to take a shortcut, which led to an unfenced swimming pool, into which I plunged. Gasping, but still determined, I crawled out and splashed my way to the washroom. I made it!

I dripped my way back to the trailer, expecting a sympathetic reaction from my family; however, it seemed I had been so wet before the pool plunge that no one could notice a difference. I collapsed into the nearest chair and my tears joined the rest of

108

the water streaming down my face and pooling around me. Carol lay feverish in the top bunk, but managed a giggle when Jack opened his birthday present: it was a pair of yellow pyjamas with "Balloon Bum" emblazoned on the back of the waistband in large black letters.

Partially recovered the next day, we headed north and in the evening set up camp just outside Montréal. No one in the camp-ground spoke English; when I tried my French, which I thought was acceptable, the other campers looked at me blankly and walked away.

I spread our sleeping bags on the grass to air and dry out. They were soft and comfortable for sleeping that night, but the next morning I awoke with swollen, crimson and itchy ears that looked like red cabbage leaves. Jack and the kids reacted with great peals of laughter. Even our unsociable neighbours looked at me and grinned.

"Poison ivy," they somehow managed to say in English.

At last we began the long trip home across the Prairies. The flat, unbroken land hypnotized us with its vastness. The kids were healthy again: Carol was impatient to see her friends and Rob was tired of persuading us to play "I Spy" and "Twenty Questions." On the last day we drove through Lloydminster. It was dry and pleasant, with some attractive motels on the east side of town.

About twenty miles from Edmonton, we found ourselves following behind a big truck that was hauling barrels. Suddenly, the chains securing the barrels gave way. They were catapulted onto the highway - directly toward us! We could do nothing but pray that they would miss us. Miraculously, they did. Half a dozen barrels clattered by on each side of the car before the truck was empty. The truck's driver roared on, either unknowingly or unconcernedly. Thoroughly shaken, Jack pulled to the side of the road and asked me to drive the rest of the journey home.

Tears welled up in my eyes as the tall buildings of downtown Edmonton came into view in the distance. As we finally pulled into our own driveway, each of us gave a deep sigh of relief. I called the *Edmonton Journal* as soon as we entered the house. "Tent trailer for sale - cheap," read my ad. We sold the trailer the next day to the first caller.

Margaret

I want to have Margaret back again. I want to hear her laugh at the inanities of the world and at her own mistakes, as she did while we were growing up. I want her to be the kind and helpful sister she was when we were younger: so tolerant and understanding of my mistakes. I want her lovely smile and sparkling blue eyes to look at me with love once more.

Margaret was my guide. Mom's death had shattered the young me; my sister brought a reliable structure back to my life. She took the place of our mother as I matured, telling me what to do and when to be home, encouraging me in my schoolwork, welcoming my first boyfriend into our house. As a daughter watches her mother, I would gaze as she sat before her mirror, brushing her shiny hair and applying makeup to her young face.

She was there for me years later, as well, crying with me after my little daughter's death. Her love was constant during this worst moment of my life.

She was my link to the past. She recounted many tales about our family's history, filling the gaps in my memory and encouraging me to record the stories in my memoirs.

Margaret was a wonderful hostess. The atmosphere at her parties was always so cheerful and the food so bounteous. I wish that I could hear her tell her friends whimsical stories about our youth once again. Recounted in any other voice than Margaret's, such stories of my childhood antics would have humiliated me; told by my sister, however, with her wry sense of humour and her gentle voice, these tales made me laugh at myself.

She was my idol. I want my memories of her struggle with that mind-numbing disease, Alzheimer's, to wash away and leave her image perfect in my mind. By the end, the disease had rendered her eyes dull and vacant. Her death was not the quick, merciful one that she so deserved. I want to remember only the whole Margaret: my vibrant, gentle sister.

111

The Sparkle of Baptiste Lake

I stretch out in a lounge chair, feeling listless. The Arizona sun radiates above me, bathing me in its warmth. My mind is drugged into dormancy. The turquoise waters of the swimming pool glitter; they are as unruffled and unreal as those in an acrylic painting. No one swims; no one dives; no one disturbs the lassitude of the sleepy afternoon. Occasionally another senior citizen lumbers along favouring her knee or her hip, and gently enters the chlorine-scented hot pool with a sigh of satisfaction. After twenty minutes or so, she laboriously hoists herself out of the water and plods off to her small and well-ordered condominium. I open one eye as she leaves; then, unmoved, I sink back into my torpor. This lethargy is addictive, almost paralysing.

A vague discomfort begins to tickle the edges of my mind: I am growing too hot. With much effort, I prod myself out of my daze and slip into the water. Although my swimming is slow and difficult, the coolness of the water immediately pricks at my memory. Suddenly, my mind is brought back to a time when my life was full of promise and joy.

I see the sparkling waters of Baptiste Lake, where my family and I passed many summers when I was young. I see myself racing carelessly along the rickety wooden pier that wobbles its way out into the water in front of our cottage. With squeals of delight, I plunge into the cold blue depths. My body is strong and lithe again, slicing through the water with the powerful strokes of the crawl or the breaststroke. My friend, also named Audrey, is stronger and more skilled than I; she swims beside me for a time, though she eventually leaves me behind. I float on my back for a few moments, fluttering my fingers gently in the water, until I have recovered my breath, and then I turn and glide toward shore. Audrey overtakes me again and waves from the beach. I pull myself out of the water and we flop, exhausted, onto our towels on the warm white sand.

We notice a vigilant mother duck shepherding her small troop of babies through the bulrushes that line the shore; under and around the pier they move, through the reeds and algae clouds. A drake, proudly fluffing his bright teal plumage, circles this swimming lesson. The softly feathered behinds of the babies point skyward as they forage with their beaks underwater. A sudden noise makes them dive down and emerge, some moments later, half-hidden among the reeds. Some white-winged gulls swoop overhead with squawks of protest at our trespass into their territory.

Having rested enough, Audrey and I jump up and sprint along the sand to Appleby's Grocery Store. We buy soda pop and popcorn, and joke around with any of the other cottagers whom we happen to meet. We stroll back to the shore where we stretch out again, basking in the benevolent sun. We read or we chatter about school, teachers, boys, or our plans for the future. By now, the sun has dried our suits, and our bodies glow pink with warmth; we run to the lake for another plunge, squealing again at the shock of the icy water. Satisfied, we scramble out of the water and speed toward our cottages.

Audrey's parents, the Falconers, own their cottage, but ours is rented. Although it is a small and dark shelter, I see it as a slice of heaven. I gobble down whatever is provided by my sisters for supper - fried potatoes with onions, scrambled eggs and bacon, hamburgers, canned chicken, canned peas or corn. We eat simply, so that meal preparation does not interfere with the pleasures of anyone's holiday.

Later, I run to Audrey's place and together we round up our friends Betty Blacklock and Velma Lewis from the lake. Every Saturday night a dance is held in the open-air pavilion on the lake's edge, and now we are skipping along to it with excitement. As the band plays "The Tennessee Waltz," we sway expectantly on the edges of the dance floor. Betty, a skilled pianist, is soon asked to play for the crowd. Then the band swings into the lively beat of "In the Mood," and we jitterbug until our breath is gone.

Thoughts of such physical exhaustion bring me back to the present, when I am dozing by the pool under the immobilizing southern sun.

These memories of Baptiste Lake make me realize that in my lazy, apathetic state I have forgotten how vibrant life can be. I push myself up onto my feet, for I am renewed and invigorated by my reminiscences. I walk off with a spring in my step and optimism in my mind. I'll go home and invite some friends for dinner; I'll gather my thoughts and add a few pages to my memoirs. Though I had momentarily lost my zest for life, I have recaptured it through these shining memories.

Photo: Heather Kelly

Audrey Weldon Reid was born in the late 1920's
on a farm near the town of Athabasca, Alberta.
She received her BEd in 1949 and taught English for
five years in a series of schools. Her husband, Jack,
was a principal and later superintendent.

In the 1960's they moved to Edmonton and she
taught at Alberta College for seventeen years. Now
retired, she devotes her time to writing stories of her
early life in Western Canada. This is her first book.

AGMV Marquis

MEMBER OF SCABRINI MEDIA

Quebec, Canada
2003